After Many Autumns

# AFTER MANY
# AUTUMNS

## A COLLECTION OF CHINESE BUDDHIST LITERATURE

Edited by John Gill and Susan Tidwell

Translated by John Balcom

*Featuring*

Hsing Yun, Emperor Shunzhi, Hongyi, Lianchi, Hanshan,
Su Shi, Li Yu, Dongshan Liangjie, Bai Juyi, Huineng

Buddha's Light Publishing, Los Angeles

© 2011 Buddha's Light Publishing

Translated by John Balcom
Edited by John Gill and Susan Tidwell
Cover photograph by Henry Chan
Cover and book design by John Gill and Wan Kah Ong

Published by Buddha's Light Publishing
3456 S. Glenmark Drive,
Hacienda Heights, CA 91745, U.S.A.
Tel: (626) 923-5144
Fax: (626) 923-5145
E-mail: itc@blia.org
Website: www.blpusa.com

Printed in Taiwan.

Library of Congress Cataloging-in-Publication Data

After many autumns : a collection of Chinese Buddhist literature / edited by John Gill and Susan Tidwell ; translated by John Balcom.
    p. cm.
  Chiefly in English with some Chinese.
  ISBN 978-1-932293-49-4
  1. Buddhist literature, Chinese—Translations into English. 2. Buddhist calligraphy—China. 3. Calligraphy, Chinese. I. Gill, John (John B.), 1985- II. Tidwell, Susan. III. Balcom, John.
  BQ1013.A39 2011
  294.3'80951—dc22
                            2011008214

# Contents

## III. SONG DYNASTY

## IV. YUAN DYNASTY

## V. MING DYNASTY

## VI. QING DYNASTY

# Acknowledgments

Buddha's Light Publishing would like to thank Venerable Master Hsing Yun and the editors of *Selected Works of Buddhist Literature*, volume twelve of the Fo Guang *Buddhism Textbooks*, upon which the present collection is based. We would also like to thank Venerable Tzu Jung, the Chief Executive of the Fo Guang Shan International Translation Center (FGSITC), Venerable Hui Chi, Abbot of Hsi Lai Temple, and Venerable Yi Chao, Director of FGSITC for their support and leadership.

John Balcom provided the translation, and John Gill and Susan Tidwell collected and edited the texts. Amanda Ling assisted with production. The book was designed by Wan Kah Ong, and Henry Chan provided the cover photograph. Our appreciation goes to everyone who supported this project from conception to completion.

# Introduction

There have been few collections that attempt the goal of *After Many Autumns*, and none with its specific scope: to collect great works of Chinese Buddhist literature throughout the history of Buddhism in China. Inclusiveness was a guiding principle of the collection. Though much of the writing is drawn from the Chan School, other Buddhist traditions and lineages are included as well. Many of the selected authors are monks, though works by female monastics are also featured, in addition to the writings of rulers, scholars, merchants, and hermits. Poetry is the dominant genre, though several prose works are also included, with several poems realized in beautiful calligraphic script, itself its own separate art form.

What the selected works share is a heritage of Buddhist themes and imagery, in all its staggering variety. The level of Buddhist content of the works vary. Some are direct, doctrinal expositions, others deal with Buddhist concerns, and some are simply informed by a Buddhist aesthetic. What makes these works "Buddhist Literature" is less determined by an investigation into each work or author's specific religious makeup, and more determined by the generations of Chinese Buddhist readers who have found wisdom and inspiration in the literature collected within.

The other feature that brings the many works included in *After Many Autumns* together is the Chinese language itself. Translation necessarily involves making decisions of interpretation, and the translation of *After Many Autumns* was necessarily complicated and multifaceted. The greatest Chinese poetry is often founded upon its ability to offer poignant ambiguity, and to invest depth of meaning into few characters. Additionally, Chinese Buddhist literature often contends with translation itself, and can be awash in Indic concepts and transliteration. Making decisions regarding how to unpack these ambiguities can be difficult, and the editors of this collection have attempted to follow a moderate path: the goal has been to make the translations sensible to an English reader, while preserving moments of mystery and litheness. When an ambiguous passage can be interpreted in a Buddhist fashion or as plain language, the Buddhist interpretation has prevailed, and explanatory notes provided to explain its significance.

## Origins of Buddhism in China

The origins of Buddhism in China are more complex than what is allowed by a single defining moment. Though historical accounts necessarily omit the gradual cultural dissemination of neighboring peoples, the textual accounts of Buddhism's journey to China have a profound impact on Chinese Buddhism's self-conception, and most importantly, upon the evolution of Chinese Buddhist literature.

The most popular narrative account of the introduction of Buddhism into China occurs in the *Book of the Later Han*. The text mentions a dream of Emperor Ming of the Han dynasty in which he sees a vision of a tall golden man. The following morning the emperor asks his ministers if they know of such a man, and is told that to the west, in India, they worship a figure named Buddha that matches such a description. The emperor dispatches an envoy to India in 64 CE to learn more, and his men return with the monks Kasyapa-matanga and Dharmaraksha along with a host of Buddhist relics and texts. These two monks go on to complete the first Chinese translations of the Buddhist sutras, of which only the *Sutra in Forty-Two Sections* survives today.

Aside from this story there is textual evidence of Buddhists in and around China even earlier. The *Records of the Three Kingdoms* mentions that by 2 BCE Buddhism was already present in the Bactrian Kingdom to the north, in what is modern-day Afghanistan, Uzbekistan, and Tajikistan, and that it was gradually spreading towards the Han capital in Luoyang. *A Brief Account of the Wei Dynasty*[1] mentions that a scholar named Jing Lu was taught the Buddhist teachings by the Bactrian envoy Yicun in 130 BCE. This account also mentions various names that Buddhists use to refer to themselves, including Chinese translations of *upasaka* (臨蒲塞), *sramana* (桑門), and *sravaka* (疏聞), indicating that the Chinese adoption of Buddhist language predated the wholesale translation of the sutras.

Following the arrival of Kasyapa-Matanga and Dharmaraksha, more Buddhist monastics came to China and began the work of translation, creating the earliest Chinese Buddhist literature. Many of these early translations are no longer extant, but notable sutras from this period include the earliest Chinese *Dharmapada*, translated by Vighna in 224 CE, and the first Chinese *Amitabha Sutra*, translated by Zhiqian in 228 CE.

---

1. Though *A Brief Account of the Wei Dynasty* (魏略) is no longer preserved in its entirety, fragments of the work are quoted in other history texts. The cited fragment is quoted from the *Records of the Three Kingdoms*.

Though not the earliest translator, by far the most significant and celebrated is the fourth century monk Kumarajiva (344-413 CE). Born in the Kucha kingdom, now within modern-day Xinjiang, China, Kumarajiva gained notoriety for his intelligence and scholarship and was eventually brought to China by the Buddhist Emperor Yao Xing to set up a translation center in Changan. As a translator, Kumarajiva was both skillful and prolific, creating translations of the *Diamond Sutra, Prajnaparamita Sutra, Vimalakirti Sutra, Lotus Sutra, Amitabha Sutra,* and Nagarjuna's *Treatise on the Middle Way,* among many others. Kumarajiva's translations are known for their clear, natural writing, and as such are often still read and chanted today, even if they have been supplanted by later, more precise translations.

Kumarajiva's translations allowed Chinese Buddhism to grow and diversify, and lead to the founding of Buddhist "schools," or teaching traditions centered around specific texts. For example, Kumarajiva's translations of the *Treatise on the Middle Way,* the *Treatise in a Hundred Verses,* and the *Treatise of the Twelve Aspects* were introduced to Southern China by Daosheng, leading to Jizang's founding of the Three Treatise School in the sixth century. Kumarajiva's translation of the *Lotus Sutra* became the basis for Zhiyi to found the Tiantai School in the sixth century as well. The importance of Kumarajiva's translations in creating uniquely Buddhist Chinese idioms and their impact on the aesthetic of later Chinese Buddhist literature cannot be overstated.

# The Chan Aesthetic

If a single source were to be identified for having the greatest influence upon the development of the Chinese Buddhist aesthetic, it would be the imagery, poetics, and lore of Chan.

The Chan School of Buddhism has its legendary beginnings with the arrival of the Indian monastic Bodhidharma in the fifth century. Soon after his arrival in China, Bodhidharma gained an audience with Emperor Wu of the Liang dynasty, a major patron of Buddhism. The emperor is said to have asked Bodhidharma the following question: "All my life, I have built temples, sponsored monastics, practiced generosity, and made food offerings. What virtue have I gained?"

Bodhidharma answered, "In truth, there is no virtue."

Bodhidharma's answer kept him from enjoying imperial favor and communicated his uncompromising views of Buddhism: there was no virtue to be gained, because all the virtue that one needs is already present in one's intrinsic nature. This concept, today more commonly called the doctrine of *Buddha nature*, states that all beings share an innate potential for enlightenment. Bodhidharma's response demonstrates the Chan penchant for turning away from external sources of success or notoriety, but it also defines another feature which would become a hallmark of Chan Buddhism: the challenging use of language.

Bodhidharma and those who came after him operated under the fundamental assumption that the universal truth of Buddhism could not be discretely defined in language, but that a wise teacher could use language and action to creatively lead people to come to their own realizations. This attitude can be seen in how "Chan" itself is defined and used. *Chan* (禪) can be defined as the Chinese transliteration of the Sanskrit term *dhyana*, a word used to describe various levels of meditative absorption of increasing depth and focus. On the surface, the Chan School can be defined by its emphasis on deep meditation. But in the popular usage and in the works of Chan writers, *chan* is an all-encompassing term that describes a worldview that is open and unjudging and a livelihood that is free and unencumbered.

While one may suppose that a tradition that views the truth as inexpressible in language would denounce writing and poetry as a wasteful activity, Chan literature is volumous. Chan writers use language that is at times illogical, ambiguous, and mysterious in service of allowing us to think beyond language and its confines to directly experience the truth. Great Chan masters are remembered in the form of *gongans*: short stories of the terse, yet deeply meaningful exchanges between teachers and students.

Master Huineng, the next great figure of the Chan School who would come to define *Chinese* Chan, is especially known for his use of language. Huineng was said to be an illiterate woodcutter, but came to be named the Sixth Patriarch of the Chan School by proving his Buddhist understanding through writing poetry.

Master Hongren, the Fifth Patriarch of the Chan School, had issued a challenge to all of his disciples to write a poem to demonstrate their understanding, and that the author of the best poem would be named his successor. Master Shenxiu, the senior disciple of Hongren at that time, wrote the following poem:

The body is a *bodhi* tree,
The mind is like a bright standing mirror;
Diligently clean it at all times,
So it does not attract dust.

Hongren proclaims that, while the poem was admirable, its author was not enlightened. Later Huineng dictated a poem of his own to a scribe who wrote it on the temple's wall anonymously:

Essentially, *bodhi* is not a tree.
The bright mirror is also not standing;
Inherently, there is no thing,
Where can it attract dust?

Huineng's poem comments upon Shenxiu's and redirects the focus towards intrinsic nature and an absolute understanding of reality. Hongren realized the author possessed great insight, and ultimately named Huineng his successor. Huineng's teachings as preserved in the *Platform Sutra* are each of this type: they recontextualize Buddhist teachings and practices in the mold of intrinsic nature. Another element of Huineng's teaching that would become synonymous with the Chan School is his emphasis on what he called "sudden enlightenment": the idea that enlightenment can occur at any moment subject to the proper causes and conditions. The experience and circumstances of these moments of sudden realization become the subject for countless poems, and the "enlightenment poem" becomes one of the defining genres of monastic poetry.

## The Chinese Poet Scholar

Members of the Chinese scholar class, aside from monastics themselves, were the greatest contributors of Buddhist literature. Scholars were expected to possess a comprehensive education spanning both the philosophical and the pragmatic, and vied for court-granted positions as military and civic advisors, county administrators, and academics through a system of imperial examinations.

First formalized in 615 CE during the reign of Emperor Yang of the Sui dynasty, the Chinese imperial examination system proceeded, with a few interruptions, for 1,300 years. Several levels of exams were administered, with local examinations given annually and more difficult regional and national exams given every three years. Of the thousands of hopefuls taking each exam, only a select few were given passing marks and permitted to participate in the next level of examinations. Scholars who passed the national examinations were granted the title of *jishi* (進士) and given high-level advisory and administrative positions.

The content of the imperial examination and the areas of study changed throughout its lifespan, but classical Confucian texts of poetry and history made up the core of the curriculum. During the multi-day examinations, students would be provided with passages from selected texts, with a few key characters removed, and be expected to reproduce the omitted characters, requiring memorization of the text. The other major component of the examination required students to write an essay or compose a poem in literary Chinese answering a question of morality or governance, drawn from the principles of a Confucian education. At the highest-level examinations, such questions would be posed by the emperor or his advisors.

Those who succeeded in the examination typically came from wealthier families with a history of civil service who were able to finance tutors to provide their children with the extensive knowledge of classical texts required. However, given that the examination was dependent on the interpretation and explication of

Confucian texts, Chinese history is abound with stories of men from humble backgrounds who are able to pass the imperial examination and lead lives of public service due to an innate intelligence and morality. Such figures are often depicted as being opposed by government officials from established families and were often subject to court politics.

The stringent requirements of the examination produced officials who were versatile, but in possession of a curious combination of attributes. While well-read in the art of statecraft and China's literary heritage, many government officials were talented writers and thinkers in their own right. The tension between government service and the need for artistic expression can be seen in the lives of several selected authors; the most notable being the Song dynasty poet Su Shi, who was twice sent away from the capital for perceived subversion in his writings.

The character of Chinese Buddhist monasticism also began to take on a different shape from its Indian incarnation that in some ways was a reaction to the life of a scholar. Rather than developing knowledge in a library or through the rote memorization of a text, a Chinese monastic acquired his education through travel. The figure of the "wandering monastic," equal parts romanticism and reality, gained Buddhist knowledge and training by visiting prominent teachers in remote mountain monasteries, far from city life. Though remote, such monastics were far from cloistered, and their written accounts of monastic life are interwoven with the sounds and vistas of the countryside.

# Notes on Translation

The overriding goal of *After Many Autumns* was to allow the reader to enjoy and benefit from the teachings of the selected works, and to this end appreciate the works primarily as literature and not as literature in translation. However, some of the more technical aspects of the translations bear mentioning for those readers interested in scholarship.

Regarding all works of poetry, special care was taken to retain the semantic content and ordering of lines found in the Chinese. This naturally produces lines of uneven length that do not always sit pleasantly on the page, but the value of being able to precisely reference the Chinese text was judged by the editors to outweigh these occasional spots of awkwardness.

Complimenting the above, the arrangement of line numbers corresponds to the Chinese text, and are meant to provide the intrepid reader with an easy means to interact with the Chinese.

The separation of longer works of poetry into stanzas is not extant in the Chinese. These separations are provided to break the poems into logical parts that are easier to read and discuss, but should not be considered features of the poems themselves.

The names of persons have been romanized in pinyin, except in instances when the Chinese name is a transliteration from another language, such as Sanskrit. The selected works encompass centuries of literature, during which several different styles of personal, imperial, and monastic names were present. In author notes, the editors chose to designate each author by a single name, judged to be the most widely used, while mentioning other important names. Names are rendered in full in author notes, including surnames and the mountain names of monastics. Any shortening or abbreviation of names in the works are rendered as extant in the Chinese text. For the sake of simplicity, the staggering variety of Chinese monastic honorifics have been uniformly rendered as "master."

When the birthplace of an author is known, the name of the modern-day Chinese province is given in the author notes, rather than its name as known in antiquity. This was done to allow the reader to gain a sense of geographic continuity without exhaustive knowledge of the ever-changing landscape of China. Place names in the works are rendered as given in the Chinese text, and their modern locations are given in the notes, if known.

Some works exist in several versions with slight variations in the Chinese. In these instances most translations in *After Many Autumns* follow the text as found in *Selected Works of Buddhist Literature* (佛教作品選錄), volume twelve of the Fo Guang *Buddhism Textbooks*, except in instances where the variant in *Selected Works of Buddhist Literature* appears to be a typographical error.

# I

0–618

# Pre-Tang Dynasty

# SHANHUI

**Shanhui** (497~569), born **Fuxi** and also known as **Fu Dashi**, was a prominent lay Chan practitioner known for his poems on Buddhist practice. Having married at sixteen, Fu Dashi encountered Buddhism at the age of twenty-five when he met a foreign monk at a local fishpond. Their conversation had a profound impact, and he spent the remainder of his life dedicated to Buddhism.

The following selections show Fu Dashi's spartan verse style and his depictions of the transience of life. His images of aging and the passage of time are used to spur his readers to practice well, and with a sense of urgency.

## The True Nature of Equality
平等實性

An empty hand, grasping a hoe.
On foot riding a water buffalo.
People crossing a bridge,
The bridge is flowing, the water is not.

# Poems on the Four States
## 四相詩

### I. Birth

Relying upon the ovum, consciousness arises,     1
    birth arises from love and desire.
In a time now past he grew up,
    today he returns as a child.
The stars follow the cycle of human life,
    red lips open for milk.
Because we are deluded to our true Dharma nature,
    we still suffer in the cycle of birth and death.

### II. Old Age

Look into the mirror and see how your face has changed,     5
    how climbing the stairs can take your strength.
You let out a sigh: now you are old,
    going forward to bow, still your body is lacking.
Your body is like a tree grown near a precipice;
    your mind is like a sea turtle longing for the ocean.
Still indulging in your outflows,[1]
    yet unwilling to study the unconditioned Dharma.

### III. Sickness

Suddenly you contract a fatal illness,
    and because of this, become bedridden.
Wife and children are silent and sad,     10
    friends dislike being near you.

---

1. 有漏: Afflictions. Called "outflows" because one's virtues escape when they flow out of them.

You suffer—pains in thousands of veins,
    groaning so that the entire neighborhood hears.
Not knowing the dangers that lurk ahead,
    you still indulge in desire and anger.

### IV. Death

Consciousness bids farewell to life,
    a wandering spirit enters the gates of death.
Countless numbers have departed—
    I have not seen a single person return.
15  The favored horse waits with a shrill neigh in vain,
    the flowers in the courtyard will no longer be picked.
Hurry and seek the supreme Way
    and avoid the four sufferings.[1]

---

1. 四方山: Literally "the four mountains," a reference to the four masses of suffering mentioned in the poem: birth, old age, sickness, and death.

# Ten Admonishments
## 十勸

I admonish you once:           1
Focus the mind and be always mindful of the *paramitas.*[1]
Diligently practice the six perfections to attain *bodhi,*[2]
Thus you will go beyond the five impurities
    and the three lower realms.[3]

I admonish you a second time:      5
Men are not to renounce the world to seek benefit.
Even if such seeking gains something for a time,
Not long from now, you will return to *Haoli.*[4]

I admonish you a third time:
As this human body is difficult to obtain,      10
    you should feel shame for your faults.
Day and night, throughout the six time periods,[5]
    be always mindful of the Buddha,
Diligently cultivate the Triple Gem,[6]
    and go to the temple.

---

1. 波羅蜜: Virtues which lead to liberation. Also called the "six perfections."
2. 菩提: Enlightenment.
3. 五濁三塗: The five impurities of time, views, afflictions, beings, and life, and the realms of hell, hungry ghosts, and animals.
4. 蒿里: Reference to a fabled cemetery in the southern foothills of Mount Tai, but also more generally used to refer to the land of the dead.
5. 六時: A Chinese system of time division which divides the day and night into six periods each. These periods encompass the entire day.
6. 三寶: The Buddha, Dharma, and Sangha.

I admonish you a fourth time:

15 Strive to do what is good.
Do not say you are young, strong, or bright;
When the end comes, where will you go?

I admonish you a fifth time:
Think of the bitterness of hell.

20 Those who seem rich and noble and appear dignified,
Will, at a time not long from now, return to the land.

I admonish you a sixth time:
It is most important not to eat the flesh of sentient beings.
If it be not a bodhisattva[1] manifest,
Then it is family from a past life.

25

I admonish you a seventh time:
There is nothing more important than the truth.
One who says "three" in the morning
     yet "four" in the evening is not a good person;
When his life comes to an end it will not be fortunate.

30 I admonish you an eighth time:
The people who eat meat are truly evil spirits.
In this life, if you take the life of another,

---

1. 菩薩: A Buddhist practitioner who has vowed to become a Buddha to liberate living beings. Bodhisattvas that have progressed far in their practice are said to be able to assume any form to teach others.

In a future life you will be killed.

I admonish you a ninth time:
Heaven and hell clearly exist.
So do not offer wine and meat to a monastic,
Or you shall spend five hundred lifetimes without hands or feet.

I admonish you a tenth time:
Admonish one another to practice with urgency.
Once your life is over you will travel the yellow river[1]—
Father, mother, wife, and child, crying in vain.

35

40

1. 黄泉: Another name for the Chinese underworld.

# MASTER SENGCAN

There are few firm details of the life of **Sengcan** (496~606). He is regarded as the third Chinese patriarch of the Chan School of Buddhism. At age forty Sengcan encountered **Huike**, the second Chinese patriarch, between the years 536 and 551, and received Dharma transmission shortly thereafter.

Sengcan is most well known as the author of *Faith in Mind*. The poem, made up of 146 four character lines, is an early exposition of Chan views of non-duality. The poem echoes early works such as **Fu Dashi's** *Faith in the Mind's Ruler*, and **Niutou Farong's** *Faith in Mind* and shows a clear influence of Chinese concepts of liberation.

# Faith in Mind
## 信心銘

To reach the Way is not difficult,                          1
One needs only have no preferences,
Just do not hate or love,
And you will fully understand.
Even a hair's breadth of difference                        5
Becomes the distance between heaven and earth.
If you wish for it to appear,
Hold not to ease or adversity.
The struggle between strife and ease
Is an illness of the mind;                                 10
Not understanding the profound objective,[1]
Tranquility is practiced in vain.
The Way is perfect, like the vastness of space,
No more and no less.
It is because we cling and reject,                         15
That it is not as it is.
Do not pursue preferences,
Do not abide in the patience of emptiness.
This kind of even mind
Fully and naturally ends affliction.                       20

To stop acting to return to stillness—
Such stillness is itself more action.
When attached to the two extremes,[2]

---

1. 玄旨: The reason why the Buddha arose in the world.
2. 兩邊: Used throughout Buddhist writing to denote various extremes, but in this instance it refers to the extremes of existence and emptiness.

How can you know the one truth?
25 Without understanding the one truth,
Both lose their potential.
To turn away from existence is to go deeper into existence.
To approach emptiness is to turn away from emptiness.

With more words and more thinking,
30 You turn against it.
With an end to words and an end to thinking,
There is no place it does not reach.
Return to the root to fulfill the objective,
Follow circumstances and lose the principle.
35 A moment of self-contemplation
Is better than the attachment to emptiness.
The attachment to emptiness is ever-changing
For all come from a deluded view.

There is no need to search for truth,
40 One need only stop such views.
Do not abide in these two views.
Be careful not to search for them.
Just having right and wrong
Creates confusion, and you will lose your mind.
45 The two develop from one—
The one also is not to be held to.
Not a single thought arises,
And all phenomena are not mistaken.

No mistakes, no phenomena,
50 Do not give rise to "no mind."

If sense objects[1] end, the mind follows.
If the mind descends, sense objects follow.
Because of the mind, sense objects are sense objects.
Because of sense objects, the mind is able to perceive.
You may know these as two,                                        55
But originally they are a single emptiness.
The singular emptiness is the same as these two,
Both contain all phenomena.

Without seeing fine or coarse,
How can there be any preferences?                                 60
The essence of the great Way is wide,
It is not easy, nor difficult.
Those with narrow views doubt,
The more one hurries, the greater the delay.
Attaching, mis-measuring,                                         65
The mind enters the evil path.
Let it be natural;
Its essence is without coming or going.

Let one's nature be in accordance with the Way—
Carefree with afflictions ended.                                  70
Bound thoughts violate the truth
And leave you tired and dazed. This is not good.
It is not good to worry,
Of what use is it to like or dislike?

---

1. Here 能 and 境 are used atypically to mean "the mind" and "sense objects," respectively. In a wider Buddhist context a "sense object" is anything that can contact our sense organs to create consciousness.

75  If you wish to enter the one vehicle,[1]
Do not hate the six sense objects.
The six sense objects are not unwholesome,
They are the same as enlightenment.

The wise know non-action,[2]
80  Ignorant people bind themselves.
There is no other Dharma but the Dharma,
Illusion leads to the self's attachments.
Using the mind, applying the mind,
Is this not a great mistake?
85  Delusion gives rise to loneliness and confusion,
Enlightenment is without good or bad
All duality is
From the self's false considerations.
Dreams, illusions, sky flowers,[3]
90  Why bother holding on to them?

Gain, loss, right, wrong,
It is time to let them go.
If the eyes do not shut
All dreams end by themselves.
95  If the mind is without differences
All phenomena are one.
Comprehend oneness' profound essence
And forget all entanglements.

---

1. 一乘: Reference to the *Lotus Sutra*; refers to the path to Buddhahood.
2. 無為: Effortless action.
3. 空華: Spots that appear in one's vision due to optical disorders. A symbol for that which is illusory.

Contemplate the entirety of all phenomena
And return to what is natural.                                    100
To put an end to all that has come before
One cannot compare.

To stop moving until there is no motion—
Such stopping is not stopping.
Two do not exist,                                                105
How can there be one?
Investigate until the very end
Without holding to any rule.
Open the mind of equality
All that you have done will come to an end.                       110
All doubts completely disappear,
And one's faith becomes strong and upright.
All things cannot be held to
Or memorized.
Spacious, clear, and natural—                                     115
Without need to expend the mind's effort.

It cannot be fathomed:
Consciousness and affection are difficult to measure.
The dharma realm of suchness[1]—
Without others, without self.                                     120
If you wish to quickly be in accordance with it,
Only say there is no duality.
With no duality, all is the same.
There is nothing it does not contain.

---

1. 真如法界: Refers to the world just as it is, without being altered or
filtered by perception.

125   The wise ones of the ten directions[1]
All enter upon this school.[2]

This school is neither fast nor slow—
A single thought, ten thousand years.
There is no place it does not exist,
130  All ten directions are before your eyes.
The miniscule is the same as the great,
This state is the end of all illusion.
The greatest is the same as the small,
One cannot see where it ends.
135  Existence is non-existence,
Non-existence is existence.
If this were not so,
There would be no need to observe these teachings.
One is all,
140  All is one.
But if this can be,
What worries would not end?
Faith, undivided;
Undivided faith.
145  Language is cut off,
No past, future, or present.

---

1. 十方: Literally the four cardinal directions, the four intermediate directions, plus up and down. More generally used to refer to everywhere.
2. 此宗: The Chan School.

# Cᴜɪ Yᴜᴀɴ

**Cui Yuan** (77-142) was a poet, scholar, and military official during the Han dynasty. Cui Yuan's artistic and scholarly advances were matched by personal and political setbacks, the most notable being his imprisonment following his revenge killing of his brother's murderer. Despite these personal intrigues, his poetry is often didactic and moralistic.

The calligraphy below of one of Cui Yuan's maxims was written by **Deng Shiru** (1743~1805), a prominent calligrapher during the Qing dynasty.

## Do Not Talk of Someone's Shortcomings
無道人之短

Do not talk of someone's shortcomings;
Do not speak of your own strong points.
In giving a gift, one must not think about it;
In receiving a gift, one must not forget it.
Choose your words carefully and control what you eat;
Contentedness is better than misfortune.
Practice with perseverance,
And long will it be fragrant.

# TAO JING

Tao Jing (365~427), also known as **Tao Yuanming**, was a celebrated and highly influential poet and government official during the Eastern Jin dynasty. Admirers of his work include the great Tang dynasty poets **Li Bo**, **Du Fu**, and **Bai Juyi**.

The calligraphy below was written by **Ma Shouhua** (1893-1977), a prominent modern Chinese artist, calligrapher, lawyer, and public servant.

## It Is Not Easy to Know People
知人未易

It is not easy to know people;
It is truly difficult to become well acquainted.
A new friendship that is plain is beautiful,
Such a one aids in times of winter.
Guan Zhong  took as he wished:
Bao Shuya was unconcerned,[1]
Their unusual friendship shone brilliantly;
Their good names remained unblemished.

1. Guan Zhong and Bao Shuya were two prominent ministers during the Spring and Autumn period. The pair are known for the depth of their friendship. Bao Shuya gave Guan Zhong a larger share of any spoils the two of them earned, as well as recommending Guan Zhong above himself.

# WANG XIZHI

**Wang Xizhi** (303-361) was a prolific calligrapher and poet whose work would rise to prominence during the Tang dynasty. Though few of his original works of calligraphy have survived, his compositions have been widely copied and collected. One particular collection of his work, the *Text of One Thousand Characters*, was compiled posthumously by the scholar **Zhou Xingsi**. Made up of 125 rhyming lines of eight characters each, with no characters repeated, the *Text of One Thousand Characters* has been a valuable tool for learning classical Chinese for centuries.

The text has inspired the work of many calligraphers, two who are represented below. The first work of calligraphy was written by **Master Zhiyong**, a Buddhist monastic who lived in Yongxin Temple in Zhejiang Province. A renowned calligrapher in his own right, he was a seventh-generation descendant of Wang Xizhi.

The second work of calligraphy was written by **Huaisu** (737-799), a Buddhist monastic and calligrapher noted for his cursive script.

## Text of One Thousand Characters
## 千字文

Accumulated evil brings disaster;
Doing good is the source of blessings.
A foot of jade is not a treasure;
An inch of time is powerful.

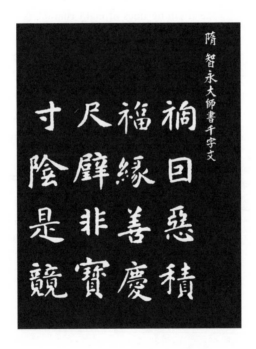

One must correct one's errors when they are known;
Do not forget what you gain.
Do not talk about someone's shortcomings;
Do not presume upon your own strong points.

# II

618–907

# Tang Dynasty

# MASTER HUANGBO XIYUN

黃
檗
希
運

**Master Huangbo Xiyun** (d. 850) was born in Fujian Province and ordained at a young age. After traveling and learning from many teachers, he eventually became a student of the famed Chan master **Baizhang Huaihai**.

Master Xiyun is remembered for his striking appearance. He was an unusually tall, imposing figure, and is said to have had a rounded growth protruding from his forehead. He had a brash teaching style, incorporating shouting and hitting to make his points. One of his students, **Master Linji**, would become well known for employing these same methods, and would go on to found the Linji School of Chan Buddhism.

He is also the author of *Chan Master Huangbo Duanjie's Mind Transmission of the Core Teachings*.

## To Free Oneself from Affliction Is Not Easy
### 塵勞迴脫事非常

To free oneself from affliction is not easy;
Grasp the rope and pull it tight until it is done.
Without it being chilled to the core,
How can we smell the plum blossom's fragrance?

香嚴智閑

# Master Xiangyan Zhixian

**Master Xiangyan Zhixian** (?-898) was a monk from Shandong Province. He lived and taught on *Xiangyan*, "Fragrant Mountain," and had over one thousand monastic disciples.

His poem "One Strike and I Forgot All I Knew" references the story of his enlightenment. Though Xiangyan Zhixian had become a learned scholar, he did not attain enlightenment early in his life as a monastic. One day his teacher gave him the *gongan* "What was your original face before you were born?" Xiangyan Zhixian scoured his library for answers, but could not find any. Disappointed, he burned his books and dedicated his practice to answering that question. One day, while working in the fields, he heard the sound of a clay tile breaking as it struck the earth. At that moment, Xiangyan Zhixian was enlightened.

# One Strike and I Forgot All I Knew
## 一擊忘所知

1  One strike and I forgot all I knew—
No more will I rely on cultivation.
I have touched the Buddha's teaching
And will not fall into skillful explanations.[1]
5  Nowhere is there found a trace,
Outside one's speech and comportment.
Those who have attained the Way from every direction
Each say they have the highest explanation.

---

1. 悄然機: Literally "quiet secrets," implying obscure or esoteric means of communication. The author is contrasting roundabout ways of communicating the truth with embodying the truth in one's behavior.

# MASTER HUINENG

**Master Huineng** (638-713) is considered the sixth and final sole patriarch of the Chan School of Buddhism. An innovative figure, Huineng emphasized the sudden appearance of enlightenment, the importance of cultivating meditative concentration beyond sitting, and the centrality of Buddha nature. His teachings have had a profound impact not only on the Chan School, but also Chinese Buddhism in general.

Born in Guangdong Province in Southern China, Huineng grew up poor and made a meager living as a woodcutter. He first encountered Buddhism when he heard a passerby chanting the *Diamond Sutra* and had an epiphany. Shortly thereafter he sought out the chanter's teacher, **Hongren**, the Fifth Patriarch. After living at Hongren's monastery for eight months, Huineng demonstrates his enlightenment by writing a poem anonymously. Recognizing the author as Huineng, Hongren transmits the Chan lineage to him, making him the Sixth Patriarch.

Though Huineng was not formally educated and described himself as illiterate, an account of his life and teachings was posthumously compiled by his disciples as the *Platform Sutra*. The "Formless Gatha" appears in the sutra, and is an effective summary of the main aspects of Huineng's teachings.

31

# Formless Gatha
## 無相頌

1  With an even mind,
      why bother upholding precepts?
  With an upright practice,
      why meditate?

To have gratitude,
      be filial towards your parents.
To be just, have sympathy for others,
      whether high or low.
5  To yield to others, whether you are honorable
      or lowly, live in harmony.
To be tolerant, do not speak of the wrongdoing of others.

If fire can be produced by drilling wood,
Certainly the red lotus will emerge from the mud.
What tastes bitter is an effective cure.
10  What is grating to the ear is honest advice.

Amend your errors and give rise to wisdom,
Defend your shortcomings and you lack
      a sage's mind.
Daily, constantly practicing to benefit others,
Attaining Buddhahood does not come
      from giving money.

15  Bodhi is found within the mind
Why bother looking for the extraordinary outside?

Listen to what I have just said and apply it—
The West[1] is before your eyes.

---

1. 西方: Amitabha Buddha's Western Pure Land, where many Buddhists seek to be reborn after death.

# MASTER YONGJIA XUANJUE

永
嘉
玄
覺

**Master Yongjia Xuanjue** (665-713) was ordained at a young age and followed the teachings of the Tiantai School. He attained enlightenment after an encounter with **Master Huineng**, and began to embrace the teachings of the Chan School.

His most notable work, included in this collection, is the "Song of Enlightenment." The poem is varied in tone: at times conversational and at times didactic; the poem has both memorable images and catalogs of Buddhist doctrine. Rife with allusions, the "Song of Enlightenment" serves as a compendium of Chan teachings, and has been celebrated for centuries among the various schools of Chan Buddhism.

# Song of Enlightenment
## 永嘉證道歌

Do you not see?  1
Practitioners of the Way live at ease, effortless,
    and have no more to learn,
They need not remove delusion or seek truth;
The true nature of ignorance is Buddha nature.[1]
The illusion of this empty body is the Dharmakaya.[2]

When awakened to the Dharmakaya there is no thing;  5
The source of intrinsic nature is the true[3] Buddha.
The five aggregates[4] come and go like clouds in the sky,
The three poisons[5] appear and disappear like bubbles.

Realize reality—no self or phenomena;
In a split-second, *avici*[6] karma is eliminated.  10

---

1. 佛性: The intrinsic potential for all living beings to become Buddhas.

2. 法身: One of the three bodies of the Buddha. The Dharmakaya is the aspect of the Buddha that pervades all of existence.

3. 天真: Literally "heavenly true," suggestive of a certain effortless purity and naturalness.

4. 五陰: Five aspects that make up the "self": form, feeling, perception, mental formations, and consciousness.

5. 三毒: Greed, anger, and ignorance.

6. 阿鼻業: The lowest level of hell where beings suffer unceasingly. "*Avici* karma" refers to the extremely negative karma that results in rebirth there.

If this is a lie to deceive sentient beings
Then let my tongue be pulled out for countless *kalpas*.[1]

Suddenly awaken to the Tathagata's[2] Chan;
The six *paramitas*, the ten thousand practices, are complete.
15 While dreaming, the six realms of existence[3] are clear.
After awakening, the universe is empty.

No wrongdoing or merit, no gain or loss—
Such things are not sought in *nirvana*.
From long ago, the dusty mirror remains unpolished.
20 Now it is time to clean and appraise it.

Who is without thoughts? For whom do they not arise?
If they truly do not arise, this is not non-arising.
Ask a mechanical wooden puppet,
If praying for Buddhahood and applying effort,
    will it be attained sooner or later?

25 Let go of the four great elements,[4] do not attach to them.
Within tranquility[5] you may eat and drink.
Conditioned phenomena are impermanent—all are empty.
This is the Tathagata's great, perfect enlightenment.

---

1. 劫: A unit of time measurement. A *kalpa* is an incalculably long period of time spanning the creation and destruction of the universe.
2. 如來: Literally "Thus Come." Another name of the Buddha.
3. 六趣: Heaven, the realm of *asuras*, the human realm, the animal realm, the realm of hungry ghosts, and hell.
4. 四大: Earth, water, fire, and wind. The Buddhist analysis of the totality of physical existence.
5. 寂滅: Synonynm for *nirvana*.

Speak with certainty, express the true vehicle.
Some will not do so, but will express the meaning 30
    through emotion.
Go directly to the source, what is approved by the Buddha.
Do not pluck leaves and search for twigs.

This *mani* pearl,[1] people do not recognize it.
Inside the Tathagatagarbha[2] you can personally know it.
With the six kinds of supernatural power[3] the world 35
    is neither empty nor non-empty;
The pearl, round and bright, does not distinguish
    opaque and transparent.

Purify the five eyes,[4] acquire the five powers.[5]
Realize—only then know it is difficult to fathom.
To see one's image in a mirror is not difficult,
But how can one grasp the moon in water? 40

---

1. 摩尼珠: A mythical pearl capable of fulfilling wishes. In Buddhist writing it is used as a symbol for the incredible value of the Buddha's teachings.

2. 如來藏: A synonym of Buddha nature.

3. 六般神: Teleportation, celestial vision, celestial hearing, mind reading, knowledge of past lives, and destruction of all afflictions.

4. 五眼: Five special types of perception which a practitioner gains through cultivation: the physical eye, the celestial eye, the wisdom eye, the Dharma eye, and the Buddha eye.

5. 五力: Faith, diligence, mindfulness, meditative concentration, and wisdom.

Often traveling alone, often walking alone,
Together, those who have attained the Way enjoy
    the road to *nirvana.*
Their discipline is ancient, spirit pure, and manner elevated.
The face is worn, but their bones are strong—
    no one pays them any mind.

45  Disciples of Sakyamuni[1] speak of poverty,
While materially poor, in the Way they are not poor.
With such poverty they are always dressed in rags,
But their minds contain the Way: a priceless pearl.

The pearl is priceless, used endlessly.
50  Benefitting beings according to their faculties, tirelessly.
The three bodies[2] and the four wisdoms[3] are realized within,
The eight *dhyana*[4] states and six supernatural powers
    confirm the mind.[5]

When the best awaken they understand all.
For the middling and lowly, even as they listen more
    they do not believe.

---

1. 獨: The historical Buddha.
2. 三身: An allusion to the three bodies of the Buddha.
3. 四智: Four supramundane types of wisdom gained by Buddhist practitioners as they cultivate their consciousness: the wisdom of perfect conduct, the wisdom of profound insight, the wisdom of universal equality,
and perfect mirrorlike wisdom.
4. 八解: Successive stages of meditative concentration.
5. 心地印: Literally "mind seal," referencing the approval and confirmation of a student's enlightenment by an enlightened teacher.

Having just removed one's sullied clothing 55
How can right diligence be taught?

Let them criticize you, let them wrong you,
Lifting a torch to set fire to the sky only makes one weary.
What I hear is like drinking sweet dew;
It melts down, and suddenly enters the incredible. 60

Contemplate evil words as merit,
They can be my good Dharma friends.
It is not because of slander that some become adversaries.
How then to express the highest loving-kindness
    and patience?

The Chan school is understood, all other teachings are 65
    understood.
Meditative concentration and wisdom are fully understood,
    not imprisoned by emptiness.
Not only do I understand this,
All Buddhas, countless as river sand, do so as well.

Roar like a lion,[1] speak fearlessly.
Hundreds of beasts hear—their skulls split. 70
The elephant scrambles and loses its majesty.
The heavenly dragon quietly listens and becomes joyful.

I crossed rivers and seas, climbed mountains,
Searching for teachers and the Way to practice Chan.

---

1. 獅子: Common symbol for the Buddha teaching the Dharma.

75 After learning the road to Caoxi,[1]
I understand that birth and death have nothing to do with me.


Walking is Chan, sitting is Chan.
Speech, silence, motion, and stillness—
    their essence is peace.
Even confronting a sharp knife, I am calm,
80 Even if poisoned, unperturbed.


How many births? How many deaths?
Birth and death, on and on, without end,
After suddenly awakening to the unborn,[2]
Facing horror or insult, how can one feel worry or joy?


85 Entering deep into the mountains, living in a *vihara*[3]
In the depths of high mountains, underneath the tall pines—
Freely meditating in this expansive hermitage;
Tranquil, in carefree solitude.


Already enlightened, no need to apply effort.
90 All conditioned phenomena are different.
If abiding in form; giving arises rebirth in heaven.
Like an arrow shot into the sky


Its force spent, it falls to earth again,
Bringing unhappy lives in the future.

---

1. 曹谿: Where Huineng taught; also used to refer to Huineng himself.
Yongjia and Huineng's encounter is recorded in the *Platform Sutra*.
2. 無生: Synonynm for *nirvana*.
3. 蘭若: Simple monastic dwelling. Hermitage.

This cannot compare to unconditioned reality,       95
Which leads straight to the Tathagata ground.[1]

Attaining the root, do not worry about the branches;
Like the pure crystal which contains a treasured moon—
If you can understand what the *mani* pearl is
You can benefit yourself and others endlessly.       100

The moon is reflected in the river, the wind blows
    through the pines;
The night is long and quiet, what am I to do?
Buddha nature and the jewel of the precepts confirm the mind.
Fog, clouds, dew, and mist are now my clothes.

The bowl that tames *nagas*,[2] a staff that separates tigers,[3]       105
Two golden rings jingle on the staff.
These are not empty symbols.
The Tathagata's own precious staff leaves a trail.

Do not seek the truth, do not eliminate illusions.
Understand that the two phenomena are empty and formless.       110
No form, no emptiness, no non-emptiness.
This is the true form of the Tathagata.

---

1. 如來地: The mental state of the Buddha.
2. 龍: Supernatural serpent. Reference to an episode early on in the Buddha's teaching career where he wins a large number of converts by confining a *naga* in his bowl.
3. 解虎錫: Reference to Chan Master Sengchou, who kept two tigers from fighting by using his staff.

The mind's mirror is clear, reflecting without obstruction.
It shines in worlds as numerous as grains of sand.
115 All phenomena appear inside.
One orb, round and bright, with no distinction of internal
    or external.

Understanding emptiness, yet removing cause and effect,
Broad, boorish action only brings disaster.
Giving up existence and attaching to emptiness is also illness,
120 Like one who escapes drowning only to fall into fire.

Abandon the deluded mind, take hold of the truth;
The mind that attaches and abandons
    swirls towards skillful falsehood.
A student who does not understand uses this practice—
He mistakes a thief for his son.

125 Losing Dharma wealth and destroying merit
Comes from such a mind.
The Chan school realizes the mind
And suddenly enters the unborn
    with the power of knowledge and vision.

A great being wields the sword of wisdom,
130 With a *prajna*[1] point and the *vajra's*[2] fire—
Not only can it subdue the outsider's mind,
But demons also tremble.

---

1. 般若: Wisdom.
2. 金剛: Refers to a mythical material that is indestructible, as well as a
weapon made from such a material.

The Dharma thunder crashes, the Dharma drum is beaten,
Spreading clouds of compassion and sprinkling sweet dew.
Wherever *nagas* and elephants tread brings boundless benefits.     135
The three vehicles[1] and the five natures[2] all awaken.

In the snowy mountains the milk is fatty and unalloyed,
Its purity produces ghee which I often enjoy.
If one nature is understood, all nature is understood.
One Dharma contains all others.     140

One moon universally appears on all waters;
All reflected moons are one moon.
The Dharmakaya of all Buddhas enters my nature;
My nature is one with the Tathagata.

When one ground is completed, so are all grounds.[3]     145
No form, no mind, no karma.
In a fingersnap the eighty thousand Dharma doors[4]
     are realized,
In a split-second *avici* karma is ended.

All Dharma words are not Dharma words,
What do they have to do with my awakening?     150

---

1. 三乘: Three different means of Buddhist practice: *sravaka, pratyeka-buddha*, and bodhisattva.

2. 五性: Ordinary people, sravakas and pratyekabuddhas, bodhisattvas, indefinite, and outsiders.

3. 地: Literally "ground," though also refers to a particular stage of a bodhisattva's cultivation.

4. 八萬門: Symbolic number representing all the teachings of the Buddha.

Unable to slander, unable to praise,
Its essence is like space: boundless.

Do not turn away from this place, forever clear,
But look for it and it cannot be found.
155　It cannot be obtained, it cannot be abandoned.
It is obtained by not obtaining.

When silent it speaks, when it speaks it is silent;
The gate of giving is open and unobstructed.
Someone asks me which school I understand,
160　I say it is the power of *mahaprajna*.[1]

Perhaps it is right, perhaps it is wrong. People do not know.
To retreat or go forward, heaven cannot measure.
I have already cultivated for many *kalpas*,
I do not speak glibly to fool you.

165　Raise the Dharma banner, establish the objective.
Clearly, the Buddha named Caoxi.
The first, Mahakasyapa[2] handed down the light—
Twenty-eight Indian patriarchs are so recorded.

---

1. 摩訶般若:Great wisdom. Also a reference to the *Perfection of Great Wisdom Sutra*, the central Buddhist sutra on emptiness and non-duality.

2. 迦葉: One of the ten great disciples of the Buddha, and the first Indian Chan patriarch.

The Dharma flowed east, entered this land;
The first patriarch Bodhidharma,[1]                                            170
His robes transmitted for six generations,[2] known the world over,
Countless descendants have attained the Way.

The truth is not fixed, delusion is intrinsically empty.
Existence, non-existence, get rid of these.
    Even emptiness is not empty.
Do not attach to the twenty teachings on emptiness.[3]                        175
A single nature is the same as the essence of the Tathagata.

The mind is the root, phenomena are dust.
Both of these are like streaks in a mirror.
Wipe the mirror clean and it will shine.
When the mind and phenomena are forgotten, nature is true.                    180

Now is the Dharma-declining age,[4] a time of evil;
All beings lack fortune and they are difficult to discipline,
Sages are long gone and wrong views run deep,
Mara[5] is strong, the Dharma is weak, and there is much violence.

---

1. 菩提達摩: Twenty-eighth Indian Chan patriarch, and the first monk to transmit the Chan School into China.

2. To signify the passing of the lineage in China, Bodhidharma gave his monastic robe and bowl to his successor. The robe and bowl was continually handed down until received by Huineng, who did not transmit it further.

3. 二十空門: Twenty different understandings of emptiness listed in the *Perfection of Great Wisdom Sutra*.

4. 末法: Period many years after the Buddha passes away when authentic Buddhist teachings no longer exist.

5. 魔: A malevolent being that embodies desire and is an adversary of the Buddha.

185 Upon listening to the Tathagata's sudden teaching
They want to smash it like a tile.
The mind acts, the body suffers.
Do not complain or blame others.

If you want to avoid *avici* karma,
190 Do not slander the true Dharma wheel[1] of the Tathagata.
In a sandalwood grove, there are no other trees.
In the deep, dense forests the lion lives.

Walking alone in the quiet forest
From which all birds and beasts have fled
195 Only lion cubs follow
All are three years old, they can roar loudly.

If a fox were to try to chase off the Dharma king[2]
It is like a one hundred year old demon opening its jaws
    to no avail.
Perfect sudden teachings, without human emotion.
200 If you have unresolved doubts, find an answer.

I am not a mountain monk who distinguishes others
    and myself,
But fear that practitioners may fall into the holes of
    eternalism or nihilism.
Wrong, not wrong, right, not right,
If you miss by a hairbreadth, you miss by a thousand miles.

---

1. 法輪: Symbol for the Buddha's teachings.
2. 法王: Symbol for the Buddha.

If right, the dragon girl attains Buddhahood.[1]         205
If wrong, Sunaksatra falls into hell.[2]
As a youth I gained much knowledge,
Studying the sutras, sastras, and commentaries.

I investigated terminology endlessly,
Entering the ocean to count the sand, imprisoning myself,      210
I was admonished by the Tathagata,
Of what profit is it to count another's treasures?

From then until now,
    I realized I had wasted my time,
For years, misguided traveling,
Nature misused leads to wrong understanding,      215
Not understanding the Tathagata's perfect, sudden teaching.

Those of the two vehicles[3] study diligently,
    but they lack the mind of the Way;
Outsiders may be clever, but they lack wisdom.
Also ignorant, also stupid,
And take the empty fist and pointing finger to be real.      220

---

1. Reference to the Devadatta Chapter of the *Lotus Sutra*, where a young dragon girl becomes a Buddha, though Sariputra, one of the Buddha's disciples, claims that women are incapable of attaining Buddhahood.

2. Reference to the *Mahaparinirvana Sutra*, where the monk Sunaksatra falls into *avici* hell for slandering the Buddha and holding wrong views.

3. 二乘: *Sravakas* and *pratyekabuddhas.*

They mistake a pointing finger for the moon.[1]
The sense organs and objects are fabricated.
Not seeing a single phenomena, that is the Tathagata.
Only then can one be called, "contemplating at ease."[2]

225　Realize that karmic hindrances are intrinsically empty,
If you do not realize, you will pay karmic debts.
Like how one who is starving cannot eat a king's banquet
Or how a sick person can meet a great doctor and not be cured.

In this world, practice Chan and gain the power of
　　knowledge and vision.
230　A lotus that blooms within flames will not deteriorate.
Pradhanasura, who broke the major precepts,
　　later awakened to the unborn;
Long ago he attained Buddhahood, and has remained
　　so until now.

The lion roars, fearlessly he speaks,
Deeply pity the ignorant, stupid, and stubborn,
235　They only know to commit great wrongdoing
　　that obstructs *bodhi,*
They do not see the Tathagata open the secret teachings.

---

1. 執指為月: Reference to an often repeated passage from the
*Suramgama Sutra:* "One points a finger at the moon to show people. Such
people should follow the finger to see the moon. Those who mistake the
finger for the moon not only lose the moon, they lose the finger."
2. 觀自在: Another name of Avalokitesvara, the bodhisattva of compassion.

Once two monks broke the precepts against
    carnality and killing,
Upali gave them only a little light,
    increasing their worries,
Vimalakirti released their doubts at once,[1]
As the sun melts snow and frost.         240

The power of liberation, beyond conception,
It is my good Dharma friend.
The four kinds of offerings[2] are given, and I do not tire.
Even ten thousand pieces of gold it deserves.

Even if one's bones became powder and the body fell to pieces,    245
    it would not repay his kindness.
Understand one sentence and surpass ten billion *kalpas*,
King of the Dharma, most supreme,
More Tathagatas than sand in the Ganges have confirmed this.

I now understand this *mani* pearl
Those who believe and receive this teaching will accord with it    250
Realize this delusion, there is no thing;
Also no people, also no Buddha.

The great universe is like a bubble on the sea,
The sages are like flashes of lightning.

---

1. Reference to chapter 3 of the *Vimalakirti Sutra*. The situation of the monks is as described in the verse; Upali explains their transgressions according to the monastic rules, while Vimalakirti states that their transgressions are as illusory as all phenomena.
2. 四事: Clothing, food, shelter, and medicine.

255  Even if a wheel of iron were grinding into my head,
My perfect, profound meditation and wisdom
   would not be lost.

The sun can cool, the moon can warm,
But even demons cannot change the truth.
An elephant pulls a cart steadily down a prosperous road,
260  Can a praying mantis block its way?

A great elephant does not travel on a rabbit's path;
Great enlightenment is not hampered by a trivial point.
Do not attempt to witness heaven along a reed.
If still you do not understand, I will resolve it for you.

# WANG WEI

**Wang Wei** (669-759) was a painter, musician, poet, and government official born in Shanxi Province. His poetry reflects the Chan ideals of seclusion and living close to nature, though he spent most of his life in service to the court. Through his civil service he became quite wealthy, and donated much of his wealth to local Buddhist monasteries.

Following the death of his wife and mother, he retired to his countryside estate and dedicated himself to writing, painting, and meditation. During this period of seclusion Wang Wei deepened his commitment to Buddhism, took refuge under **Master Shenhui**, and spent his days in the company of monastics.

Hundreds of Wang Wei's poems have been preserved, though his paintings exist only in copies by other artists.

# Visiting Xiangji Temple

過香積寺

1 I'm not familiar with Xiangji Temple.
 I walk miles amid cloudy peaks;
 There is no path through the ancient trees.
 Where is the bell so deep in the mountains?
5 The high cliffs are swallowed by the sound of the spring;
 Moonlight chills the green pines.
 At dusk, rounding a wide lake,
 Meditation quells the poison dragons.[1]

---

1. 毒龍: Symbol for mental affliction.

# Du Fu

**Du Fu** (712-770) was a poet born near Louyang, in Henan Province. He was not well known during his lifetime, so most of the details of his life must be gleaned from his poetry. Du Fu lived during uncertain times of great conflict, and his poetry is often read for historical details from the period, earning him the title of "poet historian." He fled the An Lushan Rebellion and lived in a thatched hut in Chengdu for four years, during which many of his most noteworthy poems were written.

Du Fu was a friend and contemporary of the famous poet **Li Bo**, whom he met in 744, and had a great influence upon his work.

## Thought While Traveling at Night
### 旅夜書懷

1 A breeze blows through the grassy bank,
The high mast of a ship alone at night.
A star shines broadly across the land,
The moon flows following the great river.

5 Has my fame come from writing alone?
As I grow old and sick, I should take leave of my position.
Blowing, blowing. How can it be?
Between heaven and earth, a lone seagull.

# MENG HAORAN

**Meng Haoran** (689-740) was a poet and friend of **Wang Wei.** While both were pastoral poets, Meng Haoran spent his entire life in one place, and his poetry includes many elements of the landscape of his birthplace.

While the people and places of Meng Haoran's poetry are unfamiliar to contemporary readers, his interest in his relationships and the area surrounding Mount Lumen comes through in his poems.

## Returning at Night to Mount Lumen[1]
### 夜歸鹿門山歌

1 The mountain temple's bell rings as dusk falls.
 At the ferry, people noisily vie to cross the ford at Yuliang.
 Following the sandy shore home to the village,
 I take the boat back to Lumen.
5 Where the moon shines through the misty trees,
 Suddenly, I arrive at Pang's[2] hermitage.
 Stone gate and path through the pines, ever quiet,
 Where only this hermit[3] comes and goes.

---

1. 鹿門山: Located thirty miles southeast of Xiangyang County, in Hubei Province.

2. 龐公: Pang De, a hermit who lived on Mount Lumen during the end of the Han dynasty (202 BCE–220 CE).

3. 幽人: The speaker referring to himself.

# Climbing Mount Xian with Some Friends
## 與諸子登峴山

Human affairs have their ebb and flow;                               1
Time comes and goes from antiquity until now.
There are well-known spots among the rivers and mountains,
We climb this day to the promontory once again.
The water subsides showing the shallow land at Yuliang,              5
It's cold and the water at Mengze looks so deep.
The monument to Lord Yang[1] still abides;
Reading the inscription, we all weep.

---

1. 羊公: Yang Hu (221-278) was a general during the Western Jin dynasty. After his death, a monument was erected on Mount Xian.

# MASTER DAMEI FACHANG

**Master Damei Fachang** (752-839) was a Buddhist monastic from Hebei Province and student of the famed **Master Mazu Daoyi**. He spent his later years living in seclusion on Mount Damei in Zhejiang Province.

It is said that Damei Fachang attained enlightenment upon asking Mazu Daoyi about the nature of the Buddha, to which his teacher responded, "The mind is the Buddha." The phrase "the mind is the Buddha, the Buddha is the mind," became central to Fachang's teaching.

Years later, after Damei Fachang had become a teacher in his own right, Mazu Daoyi decided to test his former student. Mazu Daoyi sent an emissary to Damei Fachang to report that he no longer used the phrase in teaching, but now said "There is no mind, there is no Buddha. There is no Buddha, there is no mind." Damei Fachang declined to change, and continued to teach using the phrase that led to his own enlightenment.

When the emissary delivered the news, Mazu Daoyi was delighted, and confirmed that his student was indeed enlightened.

# This Ravaged Old Tree Leans in the Cold Forest
## 摧殘枯木倚寒林

This ravaged old tree leans in the cold forest;
After many springs my mind has not changed.
Woodcutters pass by, but do not glance over.
Old friend, why have you come to look for me?

# Liu Changqing

**Liu Changqing** (714-790) was a government official and poet from Hebei Province whose poetry rose to prominence following the An Lushan Rebellion.

Liu Changqing's poetry is fluid and elegant, and he is considered a master of the five character line. Though Buddhist and Daoist subjects are common, his poetry also deals with loss and exile. Liu Changqing was twice sent to posts distant from the capital for dissent against the government.

## Seeing Off Master Lingche
### 送靈澈上人

Green and dense is Zhulin Temple,
Faint and far the evening bell sounds.
A straw hat carries the setting sun,
A long way back to the blue mountains.

# PANG YUN

**Pang Yun** (d. 808) was a noted Buddhist lay follower originally from Hunan Province. Though named **Daoxuan**, he much more commonly went by the name "Layman Pang." He and his family traveled widely and learned from the most prominent Buddhist teachers of his day, including **Master Mazu Daoyi**, under whom he attained enlightenment.

Though Pang Yun was wealthy, near the end of his life he gave up all his material wealth and settled at the foot of Mount Lumen. His writings are collected in the *Sayings of Layman Pang*.

# All Sentient Beings Gather from the Ten Directions
## 十方同聚會

All sentient beings gather from the ten directions,
Each to study the unconditioned.[1]
This is the place to choose Buddhahood;
Empty the mind and return successfully.

---

1. 無為: A synonym for *nirvana*.

# MASTER BAIZHANG HUAIHAI

**Master Baizhang Huaihai** (720-814) was a monastic from Fujian Province. He ordained at a young age, and was a student of **Master Mazu Daoyi**. He is attributed the authorship of the *Rules of Purity for a Chan Monastery*, a monastic rule used throughout Chinese Chan Buddhism which stressed the importance of agriculture and self-sufficiency. Baizhang Huaihai famously said, "A day without work is a day without food."

The calligraphy selection is by contemporary Taiwanese calligrapher **Zhou Liangdun**.

百丈懷海

# Liberation Comes from Not Arguing about True or False
是非以不辨為解脫

With right and wrong, do not dispute to be free.
With knowledge, study diligently to enter the gate.
With language, say less to be direct.
With affliction, have patience to attain *bodhi*.

# HANSHAN

**Hanshan**, also known as **Hanshanzi**, was a seventh century hermit and poet known for carving his poetry in wood and stone in the wilderness. Though his real name is not known, he became known as *hanshan*, "cold mountain," after the mountains in Zhejiang Province he called home. Hanshan and his two close companions, **Fenggan** and **Shide**, also spent time cultivating at nearby Guoqing Temple, where they became known as the "Three Sages of Guoqing."

Hanshan wrote in vernacular Chinese, different from his Tang dynasty contemporaries, and frequently draws upon Buddhist themes. Hanshan's poetry was collected by the government official Lu Qiuyin as the *Poetry of Hanshanzi*, which contains over three hundred poems.

# The Water Is Clear and Limpid
## 水清澄澄瑩

The water is clear and limpid,                                1
The bottom can be seen clearly;
The mind is without a care,
All things are reflected in the water.
If illusion does not arise in the mind,                      5
Then, even for a long *kalpa*, nothing will change.
If you are able to understand in this way
There will be no other side to this understanding.

# SHIDE

**Shide** was a hermit and companion of **Hanshan**. He was abandoned as a child and raised by the monks at Guoqing Temple, where he worked in the kitchen. His poems are similar in style to Hanshan's, forty-four of which are collected in the *Poetry of Hanshanzi*.

The calligraphy selection is by contemporary Chinese writer and calligrapher **Liu Zhengcheng**.

## Eliminating Lowly Words
### 除賤語

Wealth and honor are like floating clouds and
    not worth flaunting,
The ways of the common people are too extravagant.
Let me give you some advice in two words:
Diligence and thrift. This is the good way to start a family.

# BAI JUYI

白
居
易

**Bai Juyi** (772-846) was one of the most influential and prolific poets of the Tang dynasty, writing more than three thousand poems. Bai Juyi's style is simple and direct. His poetry is moralistic, but he chooses human emotions and problems as his subjects over proscribing didactic admonitions. His work was widely circulated during his own lifetime, reaching as far as Korea and Japan.

Born in Henan Province, he took the Imperial Examination late in life, when he was nearly thirty. He passed the examination and began to ascend the ranks as a government official. As he approached middle-age he embraced Buddhism, and would learn from the prominent monastics of his day.

# The Flower Is Not a Flower
## 花非花

The flower is not a flower,
The fog is not fog.
Midnight comes,
Dawn goes,
Coming like a spring dream, it does not stay long;
Going like the morning clouds, there is no place to meet it.

# A Poem on Swallows to Show Old Man Liu
## 燕詩示劉叟

*An old man had a son whom he loved dearly and who ran away behind his back. The old man was very sad, though, when he was young, he had done the same. I wrote this poem as a parable for these events.*

1  There were two swallows on the eaves,
    One cock, one hen, and they flew together.
    They built a nest between the rafters,
    And had four fledglings.

5  The four fledglings grew day and night,
    Chirping, demanding food;
    The worms were difficult to catch,
    And the babies were never full.

    Their beaks and claws wanted to give out,
10  But their minds and strength couldn't rest.
    They came and went a thousand times,
    Fearful lest the nestlings were still hungry.

    They labored for thirty days,
    Their mother grew thin, but the fledglings got fatter.
15  They tweeted to teach them to sing,
    Brushed their feathers one by one.

    One day, with wings grown,
    They flew out above the courtyard branches,

Raised their wings and never turned back.
Carefree, they scattered on the wind.                    20

Mother and father cried in the sky,
Calling, calling in vain.
They returned to their empty nest,
Sadly weeping all night long.

Oh swallows, do not be sad,                              25
You should remember and reflect,
Think of the days you were a fledgling,
And soared away, betraying your mother.
Meanwhile, your parents remember;
This day you should understand.                         30

## Wine Shared Together
### 對酒

Why do we fight over snails' antennas?
Residence in this body is like the spark of a flame.
No matter rich or poor, be happy and joyful,
Those who do not smile are the ignorant people.

# The Spring of White Clouds
## 白雲泉

The spring of White Clouds on Tianping Mountain,
The clouds are themselves empty of mind,
    the water itself is at ease.
Why charge down the slopes,
Further disturbing the human world?

# Contemplating the Illusory
## 觀幻

1 All that arises exists because of cessation;
Without being apart, there is no coming together.
Delight will end in sorrow,
Turn to suffering, and become emptiness.
5 Your eyes grow weak with age,
Soon the candle will burn out in the wind,
With no place it can be found,
As birds' tracks left behind in the sky.

# Flowers in a Monastic Courtyard
## 僧院花

The wish to become enlightened to form and emptiness
    is the task of the Buddhas.
Planting fragrant trees in the monastery,
Observing them closely,
    I saw the *Flower Adornment's*[1] verses—
The wind's skillful means blossoms the flowers of wisdom.

---

1. 華嚴: *Flower Adornment Sutra,* one of the largest and most celebrated sutras in Mahayana Buddhism.

# LI SHEN

Li Shen (d. 846) was a scholar and poet from Jiangsu Province. After passing the imperial examination, he eventually ascended through the ranks and became a professor at the prestigious Hanlin Academy. He was known as one of the "three handsome gentlemen," along with the scholars **Li Deyu** and **Yuan Zhen**.

## Pity the Farmers
憫農

Hoeing the rice field at high noon—
Sweat drips, falling to the soil.
Who knows that every grain on the
Dinner plate is the fruit of hard work?

# Liu Zongyuan

**Liu Zongyuan** (773-819) was a government official, writer, and poet from Shanxi Province. His thought and work is varied and far reaching: Liu utilized Confucian and Buddhist ideas in his writing and wrote in a staggering variety of genres. Along with contemporary **Han Yu**, Liu Zongyuan was one of the central figures of the Guwen (古文) literary movement, which sought to return to the direct, expressive writing of the Han dynasty and eschewed the florid diction and structures that were popular during the Tang dynasty.

# Viewing Mountains with Master Haochu

*Sent to My Friends and Relatives in the Capital*

與浩初上人同看寄京華親故

The coastal mountains are as sharp as swords,
Autumn comes, and all places pierce my sorrowful entrails.
If I could make of myself billions
I'd place them all on the peaks to gaze homeward.

# Du Mu

**Du Mu** (803-852) was a poet and government official born in Changan to an elite family. His work often reflects his political concerns, including a distrust of the unruly military and the corruption of local officials. Du Mu's poetry is lyrical and nostalgic, frequently recalling the past to comment upon the present.

# Spring South of the Yangze River
## 江南春

For one thousand miles there is the sound of orioles—
    reds set amid greens;
Tavern flags flutter in the breeze in river villages
    and walled mountain towns.
Four hundred and eighty temples were built
    during the Southern dynasties,
A multitude of towers and pavilions in the misty rain.

# LI AO

**Li Ao** (774-836) was a Confucian philosopher, scholar, and poet. After passing the imperial examination he became an official historian for the government. When assigned to a new post in southern China he composed the *Record of Coming to the South*, a detailed account of the southern regions and an early form of the diary. Later in life he came to know several Chan masters, and developed an interest in Buddhism.

# Visiting Chan Master Yaoshan
### 訪藥山禪師

Through cultivation, your body has come to resemble a crane,
A pair of sutra cases[1] under thousands of pine trees.
I come to ask about the Way, but nothing more is said,
Just clouds in the sky and water in the jug.

---

1. 函經: A long, narrow container used to hold Buddhist sutras for chanting.

# MASTER ZHAOZHOU CONGSHEN

**Master Zhaozhou Congshen** (778-897) was a monastic from Shandong Province, and a student of **Master Nanquan Puyuan**. He stayed with his teacher for over two decades, traveling only later in life. His teachings frequently appear in collections of *gongans*, such as the *Blue Cliff Record* and the *Gateless Gate*, including his answer to the question, "Does a dog have Buddha nature?"

# Ode to the Wooden Fish[1] and Drum
## 魚鼓頌

The four great elements come from he who built them,
It has a voice born from the emptiness inside.
They are averse to speaking to ordinary people
Only because the notes of the scale are different.

---

1. 魚: A bulbous woodblock-type instrument used in Buddhist liturgical chanting.

# PEI XIU

**Pei Xiu** (791-864) was a government official and lay Buddhist follower from Henan Province. He served as chancellor to Emperor Xuanzong between the years 847 and 860. He was very learned in the Buddhist sutras, and kept the company of several Chan masters, including **Master Guishan Lingyou**, **Master Zongmi**, and **Master Huangbo Xiyun**.

Pei Xiu was a staunch supporter of Buddhism, offering his own home to be converted into a temple and supporting his son's ordination. He collected and compiled the teachings of Master Huangbo Xiyun, and spent the end of his life living simply and as a vegetarian.

# Gatha on Transmitting Mind
## 傳心偈

| | |
|---|---|
| The mind cannot be transmitted, | 1 |
| Use a profound connection to transmit it. | |
| The mind cannot see, | |
| Use emptiness to see. | |

| | |
|---|---|
| Such a connection is not a connection, | 5 |
| Emptiness is not emptiness. | |
| The manifested city does not exist,[1] | |
| As described, the topknot contains a pearl.[2] | |

| | |
|---|---|
| "Pearl" is just a label, | |
| How can the city have form? | 10 |
| The mind is the Buddha, | |
| The Buddha is unborn. | |

| | |
|---|---|
| There it is, here and now. | |
| Do not seek, and do not work. | |
| To ask the Buddha to find the Buddha, | 15 |
| Many times more effort is spent. | |

---

1. Reference to chapter 7 of the *Lotus Sutra*, in which the Buddha describes the parable of a group of travelers going on a long journey whose leader uses his supernatural powers to create the illusion of a city so the group can rest before completing the journey.

2. Reference to chapter 14 of the *Lotus Sutra*, in which the Buddha describes the parable of a king who progressively shares the spoils of military victory with his troops, but does not offer his greatest treasure, a pearl hidden in his topknot, until the fighting is over.

Follow the Dharma to arise understanding,
And fall into the realm of Mara.
Do not distinguish between the ordinary and the sagely,
20   This is turning away from seeing and hearing.

No-mind is like a mirror
It does not seek out things.
No-thought is like emptiness,
There is nothing that it does not contain.

25   The Dharma outside the three vehicles,
In many *kalpas* is difficult to encounter.
If you can do such,
You are a hero of the supramundane world.

# Admonishments upon Sending My Son to Leave the Home Life
## 送子出家警策箋

As you leave the home life, you must make an aspiration. Seeking out teachers and learning the Way is not easy. Diligently offer incense and change the altar's water. Take care to sweep and wipe clean the Buddha hall and the Sangha hall. Do not wander about and do not play. When you leave or return, state clearly where you are going and where you have been. Do not return home every three or five days, for how then will you hear even a single sentence of the wonderful Dharma?

Respect your elder Dharma brothers, admonish your younger Dharma brothers, but do not become needlessly angry while dwelling within the gate of emptiness. Juniors and seniors should respect one another, be humble, and maintain harmony. Do not look down on others or boast of your notoriety. Clothing and food come with difficulty—they are not easy to acquire. Do not request so much of that which is delicious or fine. Your typical meal should be simple fare and vegetables. Coarse clothing, made of hemp, will come as you can get it. Honor and wealth will only grant you a purple robe,[1] but if you have the Way, what need do you have for golden treasures?

Understand the three kinds of emptiness and clearly know the four wisdoms. You should attain the first fruit—you should even attain the ten grounds. Pray to Avalokitesvara Bodhisattva and recite the name of Mahasthamaprapta Bodhisattva. While others sleep, you will not sleep. After the third watch you may sleep,

---

1. 紫羅袍: Purple monastic robes granted by the emperor to show his favor.

and as the fifth watch begins you must rise.[1] It is good to go to Sakyamuni's golden hall, relight the candles, offer fresh water, and bow to the Tathagata, asking for wisdom. Repay the kindness of your parent's nurturing and education, and the eight groups of celestial beings[2] will be pleased.

I carry sadness for sending my son to enter the gate of emptiness.
Morning and evening, you should plant wholesome roots.
Your body nor eyes should follow wealth, beauty, or defilement.
Your inclination towards the Way must persist even through the
cold of winter.

Read sutras and recite the Buddha's name
according to your teacher's teaching,
Diligently follow your aspiration, clear your mind,
and repay the four kindnesses.[3]
One day, you will suddenly fulfill your great capability
And throughout the human and heavenly realms
be a world-honored one.

North of the Yangze, south of the Yangze, the partridge cries.
I sent a son hastily away from Huxi.
Travel to where the water ends and the mountains cease,
Then naturally, turn and go another way.

---

1. 三更 五更: Ancient Chinese time reckoning. The timespan described is from eleven o'clock in the evening until three o'clock in the morning.
2. 天龍八部: Eight classes of celestial beings who protect Buddhism.
3. 四恩: The kindness of parents, teachers, one's country, and sentient beings.

# MASTER DONGSHAN LIANGJIE

**Master Dongshan Liangjie** (807-869) was a monastic from Zhejiang Province. He is the founder of the Caodong School of Chan Buddhism.

Dongshan Liangjie's *A Letter of Farewell to My Mother* highlights some of the conflicts between Buddhist monasticism and pre-Buddhist Chinese ideals of filial piety. The letter offers an interesting contrast between the emotional connections of the two individuals, and the literary examples of Confucian and Buddhist filial piety the mother and son attempt to conform their feelings to.

The poem "Do Not Seek Outside" is likely a reference to the story of Dongshan Liangjie's enlightenment. After consulting with a teacher to inquire about the *gongan*, "Can insentient things teach the Dharma?" he had not made any progress, and left. As he was leaving, he was walking across a bridge over a river, and saw his reflection in the water below, attaining enlightenment in that moment.

## Letter of Farewell to My Mother
## 辭北堂書

It is heard that all Buddhas who appear in the world receive their bodies from their parents. All phenomena arise in dependence on heaven and earth. Therefore, if there were no parents, no one could be born, and without heaven and earth no one would grow up. We all rely upon and have gratitude for those who nurture and teach us; and we are all sheltered and supported by their virtue. All sentient beings and all phenomena are impermanent, they are not apart from birth and death. Being nursed, given profound care, and raised with kindness are difficult to repay. Even if one were to give all manner of worldly offerings, one would still be unable to repay such kindness. Even if a person nourished his parents with his own blood, would that keep them well forever? The *Classic of Filial Piety* says: "Though [a child] provide beef, mutton, and pork to nourish his parents, still he is not filial." Strong ties lead to perpetual rebirth.

There is no more efficacious way to repay love and kindness as the merit and virtue of leaving the home life.[1] To ferry them across birth and death's river of affection and beyond affliction's bitter sea can repay the parents of one thousand lifetimes—it can repay one's parents' kindness for ten thousand *kalpas*. All those throughout the three realms who pay us the four kindnesses will not have been unrepaid. The sutras say: "When one child leaves the home life, nine sets of relatives will enter heaven."

I, Liangjie, forsake my place in life and vow not to return home. I dedicate endless *kalpas* of my senses and experiences to

---

1. 出家: Expression for ordaining as a Buddhist monastic.

instantly understanding *prajna*. I wish that you, my parents, can understand and be happy to let me go and not become entangled in our connection. I hope you can learn from King Suddhodana and Queen Maya[1] who, at another time and day, went to meet the Buddha. Today, now, we part. It is not that I turn my back on providing for you, but time waits for no one. That is why it is said: "If one is not to be liberated today, then when?" I hope you do not think of me.

I still have not realized the origin of my mind,
    though I have spent many springs.
Again and again, traversing this world without purpose.
Several have awakened inside the gates of emptiness,
Only I am mired in worldly dust.

With all sincerity I write this brief missive to say
    goodbye to family love,
Hoping to understand the great Dharma to repay
    my mother's love.
There is no need to cry and often think of each other,
Suppose you never came to know this person.

Beneath the crags, white clouds are often my companions;
My neighbors are the rock faces of the peaks.
I care not for worldly fame or profit,
Having forever abandoned worldly love and hate.

---

1. 淨飯, 摩耶: Sakyamuni Buddha's parents.

The teachings under the patriarch's words must be
    directly understood.
I must investigate the statement's hidden meaning.
All my relatives may wish to meet with me,
But may not until, in the future, I attain enlightenment.


## A Latter Letter to My Mother

It has been ten years of stars and frost since I, Liangjie, took up
staff, left my sweet home, and traveled south by rugged pathways
for over ten thousand miles. I sincerely hope that you, my mother,
can collect your mind and yearn for the Way. Gather your
thoughts, returning them to emptiness, and do not long for me
in my absence. Do not stand waiting, watching in the doorway
any longer. Any time events occur within a family afflictions are
gained and compounded day by day. A filial elder brother would
be obedient and catch fish, while a younger brother would care
for you and gather bamboo even amidst the frost.[1] Alas, worldly
people cultivate themselves, are filial, and conform to heaven.
The monk has the gateway of emptiness, admires the Way, and
practices Chan to repay his mother's kindness. Now a thousand
mountains and ten thousand rivers keep us apart. This single sheet
of paper, with its eight lines, expresses my heart's intent.

Ask not for fame and profit, nor scholarship,
Happily enter the gate of emptiness and abandon lay life.
When affliction ends, the fire of anxiety is extinguished,
Motherly love ends, and the river of affection dries up.

---

1. Classical accounts of filial piety, later collected in the *Twenty-Four
Exemplars of Filial Piety*, though this is not the text referenced here.

The six sense organs are guided by the fragrant wind
of precepts and meditative concentration.
A single thought does not arise, supported by wisdom.
To respond and stop my mother's mournful waiting,
Suppose I have died, or was never born.

## My Mother's Response

You and I are connected by past causes and conditions to share the love of mother and child. When I became pregnant, I prayed to the gods and the Buddha, "Give me a son." Having borne you full term, my life hung by a thread. When my wishes came true I treasured you like a precious gem. You soiled yourself, but I did not mind the foul smell. I diligently nursed you and did not tire. As you grew you began to study. Sometimes you would come home late and I would wait for you in the doorway. Your letter came, insisting that you wanted to become a monk. Your father was dead, I had grown old, and you were without brothers. Who was I to rely on? My son was intent on abandoning me, but I did not have the mind to abandon you. Once you left, I wept day and night. Such suffering, such suffering. Now, since you have vowed not to return home, I immediately accorded with your will. I do not wish you to be Wan Xiang who slept on ice, or Ding Lan who carved wood.[1] But, like Maudgalyayana,[2] I wish you to save me from the cycle of birth and

---

1. Additional references of classical paragons of filial piety.
2. 目連: Great disciple of the Buddha known for his supernatural powers. The *Ullambana Sutra* describes him discovering his mother suffering in hell, and asking the Buddha for a way to save her. The Buddha tells Maudgalyayana to make an offering to the sangha at the end of the summer retreat period, by which he relieves his mother's suffering.

death and to attain Buddhahood. If this is not the case, then I am still displeased. Understand my mind.

# Do Not Seek Outside
## 切忌從他覓

Do not seek outside,                                    1
Such is farther and farther from oneself.
Now I travel alone,
And everywhere I see waterways,[1]
Now, the waterway is me,                                5
Though I am not the waterway.
You should understand this,
And be in accordance with suchness.

---

1. 渠: Symbol for Buddha nature. Buddha nature is often described as the source of a river.

## Amazing! Amazing!

### 也大奇也大奇

Amazing! Amazing!
Insentient things speak the Dharma—Incredible!
Listen with the ears and it is difficult to comprehend.
Listen to the sound with one's eyes and you can understand.

# Li Jing

李璟

**Li Jing** (916-961), posthumously known as **Emperor Zhongzhu,** was the second emperor of the Southern Tang dynasty, one of the kingdoms in southern China during the politically unstable Five Dynasties and Ten Kingdoms period.

Only four of his poems remain, and they are commonly grouped with his more prolific and well-known son, **Li Yu.**

# The Fragrance of the Lotuses Have Faded, the Green Leaves Have Withered

*Tune: The Sands of Silk Washing Creek*

菡萏香銷翠葉殘

1 The fragrance of the lotuses have faded,
    the green leaves have withered;
The West wind blows, raising sorrows amid
    the greenish waves.
 Everything fades with the passage of time,
 I cannot bear to see it.

5 The fine rain makes me dream of Jisai,[1] so far away,
This small tavern fills with the chill of the jade flute playing.
How many tears fall for these unending regrets?
I lean against the railing.[2]

---

1. 雞塞: Poetic way of referring to 雞鹿塞, the border or frontier of a particular country.

2. 倚闌干: Commonly used image of remorse and regret. The image suggests looking out at nature from a balcony, slumped over the railing.

# Li Yu

**Li Yu** (937-978) was the sixth son of **Li Jing**, and his successor to the throne. Posthumously known as **Emperor Houzhu**, he was the last ruler of the Southern Tang dynasty before it was conquered by the rising Song dynasty. He was not killed in the conflict, and continued to live until he was poisoned in 978, likely for his poetry.

His poetry from the period following his loss of the throne is somber and nostalgic. The actual event of him losing his title is a frequent subject, and he celebrates the beauty of the land and the joy he held as emperor.

# How Can We Escape the Sorrows and Regrets of Life?

*Tune: Song of Ziye*

人生愁恨何能免

1 How can we escape the sorrows and regrets of life?
I alone am overwhelmed by love without end.
To my old country I return again in a dream,
When I awaken, tears are streaming from my eyes.

5 Who will ascend the high tower with me?
To look upon the fine autumn vista as I remember it long ago.
The past has turned to emptiness,
As if everything were a dream.

# For Forty Years My Home and Country
*Tune: Breaking Through the Ranks*
四十年來家國

For forty years my home and country;          1
Three thousand *li* of mountains and rivers.

Phoenix pavilions and dragon towers soared into the sky,
Jade trees and carnelian branches wove a cloudy canopy;
Did I ever know war?                          5

Since I was captured and became a subject,
My waist has become thin, my hair is white.

The panic was greatest the day I bid farewell at the shrine.
The court musicians played farewell songs,
I wept facing the palace maids.               10

# The Rain Rattles beyond the Curtain

*Tune: Waves Scour the Sands*

簾外雨潺潺

1  The rain rattles beyond the curtain—spring fades.
My silk blanket cannot keep me warm at night.

I forget I am a guest[1] in my dream,
And am always entertained.

5  Alone, I do not lean against the railing,
Rivers and mountains go on without end.
Parting is easy, what's hard is to meet.

Flowing water, falling flowers, spring leaves,
The heavens and the human world.

---

1. 客: Subject. He is no longer a "host," having lost the throne.

# The Flowers of the Forest Lose Their Spring Red

*Tune: The Joy of Meeting*

林花謝了春紅

The flowers of the forest lose their spring red—
    Much too soon!
Unbearable, cold rain in the morning and
    wind in the evening.

Tears run rouge red,
Kept here, intoxicated.
When will we meet again?
Life is full of regrets as the river flows east.

## Silently, I Climb the Western Tower Alone

*Tune: The Joy of Meeting*

無言獨上西樓

Silently, I climb the western tower alone.
The moon is like a hook,
A lonely parasol tree deep in the courtyard imprisons
    a clear autumn.

It cannot be severed
Or put in order. Tangled is
The sadness of parting—
    Another special flavor that remains in the heart.

# MASTER YUANZHEN

**Master Yuanzhen** (d. 890), known as **Master Lingchao** during his lifetime, was a Buddhist monastic who lived and taught at Mount Shanglan in Jiangxi Province.

Later during his career as a monastic he became abbot of Kaiyuan Temple in Hongzhou, which he renamed Shanglan Temple shortly after arriving.

## Poem on Condescending to Instruct
### 垂訓詩

1 Done, concealed, real, unreal—only you know;
Who should be asked the cause of fortune or misfortune?
In the end, wholesome and unwholesome will reach fruition,
The only difference is if it comes sooner or later.

5 At times, reflect on the content of your life,
Meditate and think each day what you have done.
Always place the mind on the right path,
Nature, heaven, and earth will not treat you unfairly.

# ZHANG ZHUO

張拙

**Zhang Zhuo** was a scholar who lived near the end of the Tang dynasty. His poem "Self Nature" is said to have been written following his enlightenment, and is collected in several accounts of enlightened laypeople.

# Self Nature
## 自性

Light shines quietly all across the riverbed;
The ordinary and the sagely share the same family.
If even one thought does not arise, the entirety appears;
The six sense organs stir slightly and it is covered by clouds.

# Cui Hu

崔護

**Cui Hu** was a scholar from Hebei Province who lived during the late Tang dynasty. His poem "Inscribed in Nan Zhuang, Outside the Capital," plays a part of a larger and rather curious episode in his life.

Once when traveling south of the capital, he encountered a farmhouse set amidst peach trees and decided to ask for something to drink. A woman answered the door and offered him a glass of water. Cui Hu was quite taken with the woman, and the incident left an impression on him.

The following year, during the Tomb Sweeping Festival, he returned to the same farmhouse to find the door locked. He inscribed the poem on the door to the farmhouse and departed. A few days later he returned and heard the woman's aged father weeping: upon discovering the poem the woman became so distraught that she stopped eating, and collapsed. Cui Hu began to cry, and the woman regained consciousnesses. The two were later married.

# Inscribed in Nan Zhuang, Outside the Capital
## 題都城南莊

Last year, on this day, I came to this door,
Your face and the peach blossoms were rosy.
But where has your face gone?
The peach blossoms still smile in the spring wind.

# MASTER GULING SHENZAN

Though **Master Guling Shenzan** (750-820) was ordained under a different teacher, he was a student of **Master Baizhang Huaihai** and attained enlightenment while learning with him. Upon his realization, Guling Shenzan decided to return to his previous teacher, who had not yet attained enlightenment.

One day, while Guling Shenzan's former teacher was studying the sutras near a window, a fly tried to exit through the window, continually hitting against the glass. Guling Shenzan then wrote the poem "Unwilling to Leave Through the Empty Door" in hopes that his teacher would attain enlightenment.

## Unwilling to Leave Through the Empty Door
### 空門不肯出

Unwilling to leave through the empty door,
Banging against the window is too ignorant.
For a thousand years, studying these ancient pages,
When will you achieve the Way?

# MASTER LINGYUN ZHIQIN

Little is known of **Master Lingyun Zhiqin**, as his poem and the details of his life have come to us through inclusion in several significant collections of *gongans*. He is said to have been a student of **Master Dawei Lingyou**. His poem, "Searching for a Sword for Thirty Years," recalls his attainment of enlightenment upon seeing peach blossoms.

## Searching for a Sword for Thirty Years
### 三十年來尋劍客

Searching for a sword for thirty years—
Many times the leaves have fallen to sprout anew.
Following one glance at a peach blossom,
I no longer have any more doubts.

# MASTER WUJIN ZANG

**Master Wujin Zang** was a female monastic and contemporary of **Master Huineng**. The *Platform Sutra* describes Wujin Zang as especially dedicated to the *Mahaparinirvana Sutra*, the sutra describing the teachings of the Buddha before he passed away into *nirvana*. Huineng hears her chanting it and then proceeds to explain the meaning of the sutra to her. She played a large part in the reconstruction of Baolin Temple, at which Huineng did much of his teaching.

## The Whole Day Spent Looking for
## Spring but Not Seeing Spring
### 盡日尋春不見春

The whole day spent looking for spring but not seeing spring;
Straw sandals worn out on cloud-covered peaks.
Return to casually sniff the plum blossoms;
Spring is already fully on the branch tips.

# MASTER CHANGSHA JINGCEN

**Master Changsha Jingcen** was ordained as a monastic at an early age, and was a student of **Master Nanquan Puyuan**. There is record of Changsha Jingcen teaching at Luyuan Temple in Hunan Province.

# Those Who Study the Way
# Do Not Recognize the Truth
## 學道之人不識真

Those who study the Way do not recognize the truth;
Like those of old, they only recognize the spirit.
Infinite *kalpas* ago it was the origin of birth and death;
Ignorant people are called inherently human.

# MASTER YONGMING YANSHOU

**Master Yongming Yanshou** (905-975) was a monastic from Zhejiang Province. He was a student of **Master Tiantai Deshao**, and is considered a patriarch of both the Fayan Chan School and the Pure Land School, with his teachings combining the practices of the two.

In addition to his synthesis of Chan and Pure Land teachings, he worked with prominent figures of other Chinese Buddhist Schools to compile the *Mirror Record of Transmission*, a text containing two hundred biographies of the great monastics of the past, stretching all the way back to India.

# Living in the Mountains
## 山居詩

1 Take it easy when you are busy,
   work more when you are not;
After one is not mired in worldly affairs,
   the Way goes through.
Clearly, understanding comes from beyond
   the dark nether world,
The mind is emptied among the peaks.
5 Spring waters fly over the stones without ceasing,
Clouds cover the mountains,
   then reveal their endlessness.
Though the woodcutter and fisherman seem at ease,
They do not truly dwell as I do.

# III

960–1279

# Song Dynasty

# FAN ZHONGYAN

范
仲
淹

**Fan Zhongyan** (989-1052) was a writer, poet, and government official from Jiangsu Province. Fan Zhongyan grew up in a Buddhist monastery, where he learned the Dharma and assiduously kept the precepts. In his later career as a government official he continued to study and consult with Chan masters and was a major patron of the sangha. After holding a variety of offices, he served as the chancellor to **Emperor Renzong**, where he instituted many reforms.

Fan Zhongyan was sent away from the capital on two occasions: once as a punishment against perceived subversive behavior, and once to aide in protecting the northern border. The Chinese borderlands are often a subject for his poetry. His work is collected in *The Writings of Fan Wenzheng Gong*.

# Autumn Thoughts

*Tune: A Fisherman's Pride*

秋思

1   On the frontier autumn comes, the scenery changes.
The cranes of Hengyang[1] leave, not wishing to stay.

The bugles sound throughout the border region,
Within a thousand peaks.
5   A long wisp of smoke, a sunset. A lonely city closes.

Gulping down a cup of wine,
thinking of home ten thousand *li* away;
Yanran[2] is still unconquered,
so there are no plans to go home.

A Qiang[3] flute is heard far and distant,
frost covers the ground,
One cannot sleep.
10  The general's hair grows whiter; the soldiers weep.

---

1. 衡陽: City in central Hunan Province. Indicates migratory cranes, returning south.
2. 燕然: Region near the northern Chinese border with Mongolia.
3. 羌: Chinese minority group that lives mostly in northwest Sichuan Province.

# Su Shi

**Su Shi** (1036-1101), also known as **Su Dongpo**, was a writer, poet, government official, and one of the most celebrated figures of the Song dynasty. Born in Sichuan Province, he passed the highest rank of the imperial examination at the extremely young age of nineteen, beginning his career of civil service. Su Shi was twice exiled to governmental posts far from the capital for writings deemed critical of the state, though it is during these periods that many of his most well-known poems were written.

Su Shi's poems are known for their power and forcefulness. Over two thousand survive today, variously collected.

## Recalling Minchi[1] with My Brother Ziyou
### 和子由澠池懷舊

1 Running everywhere, to what can life be compared?
  Like a crane treading in snow,
  It might leave tracks in the snow.
  After the crane has flown, does it remember east or west?
5 The old monk died, a new stupa was built,
  No traces of our poems can be found on the ruined walls.
  Do you recall those mountainous paths?
  The way is long, the traveler exhausted,
    the crippled donkey cries.

---

1. 澠池: County in Henan Province.

# Written on a Wall in Xilin Temple
## 題西林壁

*Editor's Note: The following three poems are sometimes read as part of a cycle describing the experience of enlightenment. "Written on a Wall in Xiling Temple" describes an unenlightened state, "Misty Rain on Mount Lu" describes a practitioner who has achieved concentration through meditation, and "Gatha for Donglin Temple on Mount Lu" describes an enlightened state.*

It's a mountain range when viewed horizontally,
    a peak vertically;
Near, far, high, or low—how its appearance varies.
One cannot know the true nature of Mount Lu;[1]
For one is on that very mountain itself.

---

1. 盧山: Mountain in northern Jiangxi Province. Its beauty has inspired generations of Chinese poets.

## Misty Rain on Mount Lu
### 盧山煙雨

Misty rain over Mount Lu and the waves of Zhejiang,
Missing out on such marvels brings a thousand
    unbearable regrets;
But upon actually seeing them, there is nothing really there:
Just misty rain over Mount Lu and the waves of Zhejiang.

# Gatha for Donglin Temple on Mount Lu
## 廬山東林寺偈

The sounds of the rippling creek are all words
    of the Buddha;
The mountain scene is none other than the body
    of the Dharma.
Night falls, and one contemplates eighty-four
    thousand verses,
Just how will I tell others these truths at some later time?

## Seeing Off Wang Zili with Water from Bodhisattva Springs in Wuchang
### 武昌酌菩薩泉送王子立

I have no wine or money to see you off,
So let's have a cup of water from Bodhisattva Springs.
Lower your head in any place and you will see me,
The water in the four directions reflects the same sky.

# Recollections of the Red Cliffs[1]

*Tune: The Charm of Niannu*

赤壁懷古

The river flows east;                                               1
Its waves wash away
All the awe-inspiring heroes of old.

West of the ancient fortress
They speak of                                                        5
The Three Kingdoms's Zhou[2] at the Red Cliffs.

Flying rocks shatter the clouds,
Frightful waves strike the shore,
Rising like a thousand heaps of snow.

Rivers and mountains like a painting—                               10
A time of so many heroes!

I think of Zhou Yu at that year,
Young lady Qiao,[3] newly married.
Dashing and clever.

---

1. 赤壁: Site of a decisive battle during the Three Kingdoms period; a period whose generals and military heroes have since been immortalized in literature and the popular imagination.

2. 周: Zhou Yu (175-210), one of the major generals of the Kingdom of Wu.

3. 小喬: Wife of Zhou Yu. Known for her beauty.

15 A feathered fan flutters, blue silken headband;
Between chatting and smiling.
The Wei[1] army, now ash in the wind, gone up in smoke.

I think of the old country.
You laugh at me for being too sentimental,
20 With white hair before my time.
Life is like a dream,
Offering a cup of wine to the moon in the river.

---

1. 魏: Northern kingdom during the Three Kingdoms period and op-
ponent of Zhou Yu and the states of Wu and Shu.

# Composed While Residing at
# Dinghui Monastery in Huangzhou

*Tune: The Diviner*

黃州定惠院寓居作

A wan moon hangs over a parasol tree                    1
The water clock, silent. Everyone in bed.
Who sees the hermit come and go alone?
Vague and unnoticed, a lone crane's shadow.

Startled, it turns and looks                            5
No one knows its regrets,
Unwilling to choose any withered branch to rest,
Lonely on the cold, sandy bank.

# When Does the Bright Moon Appear?

*Tune: Prelude to Water Music*
明月幾時有

*Mid-autumn, 1076. I drank till the sun came up and got very drunk. I missed my brother Ziyou and wrote these lyrics.*

1 When does the bright moon appear?
I lift my cup and ask the night sky:
Do you know, in heaven's court,
What year it is?

5 I would ride the wind and wend my way there,
But I fear the carnelian towers and the jade halls.
I cannot stand the cold in such lofty places.

I rise and dance with my shadow,
What is it like in the human world?
10 The moon goes round the red chambers,
The gauzy windows,
Shinning on the sleepless.
You should have no regrets.
Why is it always full when we are apart?

15 People have sorrow and joy, meetings and departures;
The moon is bright and dim, full and waning.
There was nothing perfect since the past,
But I hope that humans can live long
And enjoy the beauty of the moon,
    though it is a thousand *li* away.

# Listen Not to the Pitter-Patter
# of the Rain on the Leaves
### Tune: Stable Wind and Waves
### 莫聽穿林打葉聲

*On March 7th, we encountered rain on the road to Shahu.¹ The rain gear had already been sent ahead, and the travelers were in dire straits. I alone did not care. Later, after it cleared, I wrote these lyrics.*

Listen not to the pitter-patter of the rain on the leaves;     1
Why not sing while walking slowly?
A bamboo cane and straw sandals
    are lighter than riding a horse;
What is there to fear?

I'd wear a straw cloak throughout a life of mist and rain.     5
The chilly spring breeze awakens me from my tipsiness—
A little cold.
The setting sun atop the mountain welcomes me.

Turning my head, I see the dreary beaten way I came;
Going back
There is no wind and rain, nor bright sun.     10

---

1. 沙湖: Located thirty miles southeast of Huangzhou, Hubei Province. This dates the poem to the period of time when Sushi was punitively sent away from the capital.

# Ten Long Years Obscure
# the Living from the Dead

*Tune: The River Town*

十年生死兩茫茫

*In the year 1075 on the night of January 20th, I had the following dream:*

1  Ten long years obscure the living from the dead.
No need to think upon it,
I cannot forget

Your solitary grave a thousand miles away.
5  Unable to express my sadness to anyone,

Even if we met, you probably wouldn't recognize me:
My face is weather beaten,
My hair white as frost.

Last night I dreamt I returned to my hometown
10  And saw you sitting by the window
Brushing your hair and applying makeup.

We watch each other and say nothing,
Thousands of tears streaming down our cheeks.

I think of the years of sadness.
15  On this moonlit night
On this pine covered hill.

# WANG ANSHI

**Wang Anshi** (1021-1086) was a government official, philosopher, and poet from Jiangxi Province. His career as chancellor was marked by reform, including reduction of taxes and forced labor, as well as the establishment of social welfare programs. His reforms were met with resistance from other officials, and he eventually fell out of favor.

Wang Anshi's poetry is collected in the *Works of Linchuan*, named for the county of his birth.

# Climbing Feilai Peak[1]
## 登飛來峰

There is a tower on Feilai Peak more than
    eight thousand meters high.
I have heard one can see the sun rise as the cock crows.
Fear not that clouds might block the view,
Because one stands at the highest level.

---

1. 飛來峰: One of the highest points on Mount Wulin, home to many
Buddhist temples and Buddhist rock face relief sculptures.

# Yi and Lu Were Two Old Men

*Tune: Waves Scour the Sands*

伊呂兩衰翁

Yi and Lu[1] were two old men;                                                              1
They had experienced successes and failures:
One was a fisherman, the other a farmer.
If they had not met their sovereigns,
How wasted these heroes would have been.                                            5

Tang and Wu[2] met them by chance;
They became the influential men of the hour,
Assisting their king successfully with ease.
Now, a thousand years later,
No one can match them for merit.                                                          10

---

1. 伊呂: Yi Yin and Lu Shang, two chancellors from humble back-grounds. Yi Yin was an advisor to King Tang of the Shang dynasty, while Lu Shang was an advisor to the kings Wen and Wu of the Zhou dynasty.

2. 湯武: King Tang of the Shang dynasty and King Wu of the Zhou dynasty.

# HUANG TINGJIAN

**Huang Tingjian** (1045-1105) was a writer, poet, calligrapher, and government official from Jiangxi Province. He was also a dedicated lay Buddhist follower. Huang Tingjian traveled to Shangu Temple in Anhui Province to learn Chan Buddhism, and started using the penname **Shangu Daoren**. Later in life he lived in solitude to practice Pure Land Buddhism, calling himself **Old Man Fu**.

His poetry is collected in the *Lyrics of Shangu.*

# Where Has Spring Gone?

*Tune: Pure Serene Music*

春歸何處

Where has spring gone?            1
Lonely, there is no way to go.
If someone knows where spring has gone,
Have them call it back to stay.

Has spring left no trace? Who knows?     5
Unless the oriole is asked,
But no one can decipher its warbling
Because the wind has blown it over the roses.

# All the Generals Talked about Obtaining High Rank

### Tune: The Southern Country

## 諸將說封侯

*An impromptu work composed at a party in the meeting hall at Yizhou on the Double Ninth Festival.[1]*

1  All the generals talked about obtaining high rank;
A bit of flute, lengthy songs. Alone,
    I lean against the railing.

All things have gone with wind and rain.
Gone, gone,
5  Are the golden-bridled horses of Ximatai.[2]

Drink up; but do not delay.
The wine this autumn tastes the same as last autumn,

The flowers laugh at this old man's[3] head
For shame, for shame!
10  This old man can't end his worries, even with
    flowers in his white hair.

---

1. 重陽日: An ancient Chinese holiday observed annually on September 9th.

2. 戲馬台: A city used to train horses for battle centuries before the author's birth.

3. 老人: The author referring to himself.

# OUYANG XIU

**Ouyang Xiu** (1007-1072) was a writer and historian from Jiangxi Province. For most of his life he denigrated Buddhism, with large parts of his *Benlun* and *New History of the Five Dynasties* dedicated to criticizing the religion and minimizing its importance. However, later in life he embraced Buddhism and became a devout lay follower, calling himself **Layman Liuyi**.

His poetry of this period is collected in the text *Lyrics of Liuyi*.

# Deep, Deep is the Courtyard. How Deep?

*Tune: Butterflies Romancing the Flowers*

庭院深深深幾許

1　Deep, deep is the courtyard. How deep?
　The willows loom in hazy layers
　As if separated by screen windows.

　Sightseeing, riding a horse with jade bridle and carved saddle;
5　The towers are so high I can no longer find Zhangtai street.[1]

　A heavy storm in late March;
　The door is tightly shut at dusk.
　Spring cannot be made to stay.

　Tears in my eyes, I ask the flowers, but they do not speak;
10　In disordered array they fly past the swing.

---

1. 章臺路: Street leading into Changan, the capital city.

# MASTER FENYANG WUDE

汾陽無德

**Master Fenyang Wude** (974-1024), known as **Master Shanzhao** during his lifetime, was a monastic from Shanxi Province. A gifted youth, he ordained at a young age and traveled to learn from seventy-one teachers, eventually attaining enlightenment under **Master Shoushan Xingnian**.

After the death of his teacher, he was invited to stay at Taizi Temple in his native Shanxi Province. He would remain there for thirty years, and became respected as a versatile teacher and writer. The selection, "The Song of Right and Wrong," is collected in the *Sayings of Chan Master Fenyang Shanzhao*.

# Song of Right and Wrong
## 是非歌

1 One who leaves home to learn the Way should know:
  In the monastic assembly be sure not to violate the order.
  Be kind and respectful to those who explain the truth
      and are virtuous.
  Do not associate with fools who gossip.

5 Hear one speak well of you and your mind is joyful;
  Hear one speak ill of you and hate him to death.
  Good and evil both come from the mind,
  Seek the course of reason in between.

  Worldly people are more lacking in wisdom,
10 They do not attempt to understand or think, and gossip arises.
  A great, wise person looks at it
  And does not get involved.

  Zilu was scolded when he encountered a fisherman.[1]
  Confucius once felt shame for forgetting to wear his shoes.
15 The first thing recorded about Sariputra
  Was how he was personally fooled by a fool.[2]

---

1. Reference to *Zhuangzi*, where Confucius scolds his disciple Zilu for
not recognizing a humble fisherman as a sage.

2. Reference to a past life of Sariputra, a great disciple of the Buddha.
As a monk he encounters a man who says his mother is dying, and that
only medicine made from a monk's eyeball can cure her. Sariputra plucks
out his eye, but the man says that only the *right* eyeball will do. Having
removed his left, the monk then removes the other eye. The man smells
the eye, says it is too smelly to be medicine, and crushes it.

The Tathagata looks at all sentient beings with his eyes
    of compassion,
He knows the past and present, and clearly sees the truth.
These dynasties—Zhou, Qin, Han, and Wei,
Each of these countries was destroyed for the same reason.[1]    20

For many *kalpas*, gossip has been the cause of hell,
When you hear or speak of right and wrong,
    examine the details.
I hear it spoken, my mind does not arise—
This is gossip. It stops at me.

Still, there are some empty words that cannot be polished;    25
To ask for what reason the patriarch came from the west.
If you wish for clarity, to be able to distinguish the roots
    from the branches,
Understand the true basis of gossip.
More people come to speak gossip,
But now I already recognize you.    30

---

1. The end of each dynasty was accelerated by some form of infighting.

## Poem in Praise of Coming from the West
### 西來意頌詩

Cypress trees grow up from the land in the courtyard.
There is no need for ox or plow to till this peak.
This is the right way to teach the one thousand roads
    from the west.[1]
The dense, dark woods all have eyes.

---

1. 西來種千路: Many methods for teaching the Dharma. "West" is a reference to India, and one thousand to the multiplicity of teachings.

# MASTER WUZU FAYAN

五祖法演

**Master Wuzu Fayan** (d. 1104) was a monastic from Sichuan Province. Wuzu Fayan initially studied the Consciousness-Only teachings, but when they failed to lead him to enlightenment he sought out Chan teachers, eventually attaining enlightenment under **Master Baiyun Shouduan**. After learning and teaching in several temples, he settled on Mount Wuzu and took up residence in Dongchan Temple.

"Of the Fallow Field before the Mountain" is collected in the *Record of the Jiatai Era's Transmission of the Lamp*.

## Of the Fallow Field before the Mountain
山前一片閑田地

Of the fallow field before the mountain,
With folded arms, I inquire of an old man.
Many times it has been sold, and still it is sold.
Why not enjoy the bamboo, pines, and breeze?

天
衣
如
哲

# MASTER TIANYI RUZHE

Little is known of **Master Tianyi Ruzhe** (d. 1160), except for the most basic details regarding his place in the Chan lineage. Tianyi Ruzhe was ordained in the Yunmen School, and his teacher was **Master Jingzhao Chongxin**.

His poem "Ruiyan Always Said, 'Master, Are You Awake?'" references the Tang dynasty Chan master **Ruiyan Shiyan**. Ruiyan Shiyan was known for saying aloud, "Master, are you awake?" and then answering himself, "Yes, yes," to affirm his mindfulness. The poem is collected in the *Record of the Jiatai Era's Transmission of the Lamp*.

## Ruiyan Always Said,
## "Master, Are You Awake?"
### 瑞巖常喚主人公

Ruiyan always said, "Master, are you awake?"
Standing atop Sumeru's highest peak,
Turning the world over, nowhere to be found,
But in a single flute song in a beautiful hall.

# Sima Guang

**Sima Guang** (1019-1086) was a scholar, historian, and government official from Shanxi Province. Though he held a variety of governmental posts, Sima Guang is most well known for his history writing. His greatest work, the *Mirror to Aid in Governance* attempted to document the complete history of China at that time, and is over three million characters in length.

The selected poem is an example of one of Sima Guang's maxims, and the calligraphy is written by **Zhuang Dong**.

司馬光

# Family Teachings
## 家訓

Accumulate gold for your descendents,
And your descendents might not save it.
Accumulate books for your descendents,
And your descendents might not read them.
It would be better to privately accumulate merit
    for them in this life
To make long-term plans for them.
This is a maxim of the ancient sages
And something for later generations to think upon.

# ZHANG ZAI

**Zhang Zai** (1022-1077) was a philosopher and government official from Shanxi Province. He wrote extensively on Confucian morality and cosmology, and composed a notable commentary on the *Book of Changes*.

The calligraphy is written by contemporary Taiwanese calligrapher **Li Chaozai**.

# Devote Your Mind to Heaven and Earth
## 為天地立心

Devote your mind to heaven and earth;
Devote your life to the people.
Succeed the wisdom of the past sages;
Create peace for ten thousand generations.

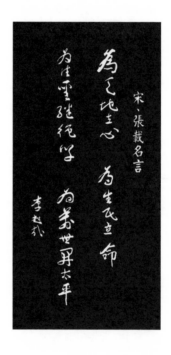

# MASTER BAIYUN SHOUDUAN

**Master Baiyun Shouduan** (1025-1072) was a monastic from Hunan Province. He ordained under **Master Chalingyu** in the Linji School of Chan Buddhism, though he would attain enlightenment while learning from **Master Yangqi Fanghui** and became his successor. Baiyun Shoudan traveled and taught widely, living and teaching as far north as the Longmen mountains in Henan Province and as far south as Mount Baiyun in Guangdong Province.

The selected poems are taken from the *Sayings of Chan Master Baiyun Shouduan*, and recall Baiyun Shouduan's moment of enlightenment when setting foot onto a bridge.

白雲守端

## Concerning the One Hundred Foot Pole, I Have Made Progress

### 百尺竿頭曾進步

Concerning the one hundred foot pole,[1]
  I have made progress
With one step onto a bridge, all the mountains and
  rivers disappeared.
Since then, I have not left chachuan;[2]
Even singing out is not inexcessive speech.

---

1. 百尺竿: Reference to "sitting atop a one hundred foot pole," a metaphor for accomplishing a difficult task, in this case attaining enlightenment.

2. 茶川: Literally "tea river."

# For Love I Seek the Light by Pouring over Books
## 為愛尋光紙上鑽

For love I seek the light by pouring over books;
I was unable to leave that place—how difficult.
Suddenly, I arrive on the road I came from
And begin to awaken to the past my eyes had cheated
    from me.

石頭
頭
懷
志

# MASTER SHITOU HUAIZHI

**Master Shitou Huaizhi** (1040-1103) was a monastic from Zhejiang Province. He was ordained in the Linji Chan School by **Master Baofeng Kewen**.

His poem "At Rest from a Myriad Affairs, Foolishness Takes Over," is collected in the *Record of the Jiatai Era's Transmission of the Lamp*.

# At Rest from a Myriad Affairs, Foolishness Takes Over
## 萬機休罷付癡憨

At rest from a myriad affairs, foolishness takes over.
When there are tracks, a wild deer is nearby;
Sleeping in my rough hemp clothes, my fist as a pillow,
Many lives dreaming in a green hut.

# MASTER CONGYUE

**Master Congyue** (1044-1091) was a monastic from Jiangxi Province. He was ordained in the Linji Chan School by **Master Baofeng Kewen** and became his successor. He became an accomplished writer, poet, and leader who was praised far and wide. He was posthumously awarded the honorary title of "Master True Tranquility" by Emperor Huizong of the Song dynasty, under the recommendation of Chancellor Zhang Shangying.

His poem "When I Practice at Ease" is collected in the *Unified Record of the Transmission of the Lamp*. A collection of Congyue's teachings has also been preserved in the text *Essential Sayings of Chan Master Doushuai Yue.*

# When I Practice at Ease
## 等閑行處

When I practice at ease,                                    1
Every step is like this.
Though I dwell on sound and form,
Have I been hindered?

One mind without differentiation;                           5
All phenomena are not special.
Do not distinguish essence and function,
Nor choose between fine and coarse.

Unhindered by any situation,
Free to respond to all things.                              10
Right and wrong are without emotion,
Ordinary and sagely, all eliminated.

Who wins and who loses?
What is close and what distant?
Mistake a head for a tail;                                  15
Point out truth as illusory.

Overturn the realm of Mara;
Turn one's feet away from the evil path.
Understanding is not easy or difficult;
There is no need for any effort.                            20

# MASTER YUANWU KEQIN

**Master Yuanwu Keqin** (1063-1135) was a monastic from Sichuan Province. He was a student of **Master Fayan**, and lived and taught at Lingquan Temple on Mount Jia. Yuanwu Keqin edited the *Blue Cliff Record*, a massively influential text that collected and commented upon one hundred of **Master Xuedou Chongxian's** poems on the lives and teachings of previous Chan masters. The *Blue Cliff Record* served as a compendium of essential Chan teachings and shaped the Chan discourse as the school continued to develop in China and throughout Asia.

In the year 1111, **Emperor Huizong** offered him a purple robe and an imperial title, and Yuanwu Keqin relocated to the capital. He continued to enjoy favor under the subsequent emperor, and was later given the posthumous title of Zhenjue, "Truly Awakened."

His poem "A Golden Duck upon a Pillow, Splendid Curtains" is collected in the *Record of the Jiatai Era's Transmission of the Lamp*. His teachings are compiled in the twenty-volume *Sayings of Chan Master Yuanwu Foguo*.

# A Mandarin Duck upon a Pillow, Splendid Curtains
## 金鴨香囊錦繡幃

A Mandarin duck[1] upon a pillow, splendid curtains,
Dense with music and song, drunkenly clinging together—
The romances of youth,
Are only for the beautiful to know.

---

1. 金鴨: Symbol for marriage, as Mandarin ducks mate for life. The image suggests a newly wed couple.

# Master Longmen Qingyuan

**Master Longmen Qingyuan** (1067-1120) was a monastic from Sichuan Province. He ordained in the Linji Chan School under **Master Wuzu Fayan**. He lived much of his life in seclusion on Mount Simian, until traveling to Longmen where he began to gather disciples.

His poem "In the Daodao Forest, the Birds Sing," is collected in the *Record of the Jiatai Era's Transmission of the Lamp*, and references the story of his enlightenment. One rainy night Longmen Qingyuan was reading *Transmission of the Lamp*. As he stoked his campfire he read the biography of **Master Pozaoduo**, who once denounced a communal cooking stove that was worshiped by the local people, decrying its participation in the destruction of so many animals' lives. The stove then fell over, revealing a deity who thanked Pozaoduo for liberating him through his teaching. Upon reading this entry, Longmen Qingyuan attained enlightenment.

# In the Daodao Forest, the Birds Sing
## 刀刀林鳥啼

In the Daodao Forest, the birds sing.                           1
Sitting wrapped in a cloak all night,
Poking the fire, I awaken to life.
Having spent all my energy, a breakthrough:

Everything is clear, it is people who delude themselves;        5
Who can harmonize a simple tune?
Think of this and remember it always:
The door is open, but few pass through.

# MASTER XINGKONG MIAOPU

性
空
妙
普

**Master Xingkong Miaopu** (1071-1142) was a monastic from Sichuan Province. He ordained in the Linji Chan School and was a student of **Master Sixin Wuxin**. Xingkong Miaopu lived in a thatched hut that he built himself along the bank of the Qinglong River, and he would spend his days playing the flute and writing didactic verse.

His selected poems are collected in *Record of the Jiatai Era's Transmission of the Lamp*. Both reference Xingkong Miaopu's admiration for the ninth century monastic **Master Chuanzi**. Chuanzi was a student of **Master Yaoshan Weiyan**, and was known for frequenting ferries and using light conversation to teach the Dharma to those onboard.

## When Chuanzi Went Home That Year
### 船子當年返故鄉

When Chuanzi went home that year
He left leaving no trace—It was quite wonderful.
His true wind[1] blew across to those who understood him
Playing his iron flute as he departed.

---

1. 真風: Metaphor for the influence of a person's virtuous conduct.

## Liberation While Sitting or
## Dying While Standing
### 坐脫立亡

1  Liberation while sitting or dying while standing
Cannot compare to a water burial:[1]
First benefit: save on firewood.
Second benefit: no grave to dig.

5  Let go and set off—
How happy and wonderful!
Who truly understands me?
The monk Chuanzi.

It will be difficult for his virtuous wind to succeed
for 100,000 years;
10  A fishing song that few sing.

---

1. 水葬: Burial practice attributed to several Chan masters. Through deep meditation they discern that they only have moments left to live. They then take a small boat out to sea and break a hole in the hull, sinking the boat. This is done so that others will not have to care for their bodies after death.

# Master Huaishen Cishou

**Master Huaishen Cishou** (1077-1132) was a monastic from Anhui Province. He ordained in the Yunmen Chan School and was a student of **Master Changlu Chongxin**, and would eventually become his successor at Zisheng Temple located in Zhejiang Province.

At the turn of the twelfth century, he was requested by the government to relocate to Jiaoshan in Jiangsu Province and later to Huilin Temple in Luoyang to be closer to the capital. In 1127, soldiers from the Jin dynasty besieged the Song capital of Kaifeng. Huaishen Cishou twice asked to be relieved of his duties as National Master, finally relocating to a cave on Mount Bao.

His poem "I Only Travel to Old Places I Have Been" is collected in the *Record of the Jiatai Era's Transmission of the Lamp.* "Undergoing Ten Thousand Things Cannot Compare to One Who Retreats" appears in the compiled collection of his teachings, *Sayings of Master Huaishen Cishou.*

## I Only Travel to Old Places I Have Been
只是舊時行履處

I only travel to old places I have been,
Carelessly forming attachments. Such is confusion.
A strong wind rises at night,
Blowing down many peach blossoms.

# Undergoing Ten Thousand Things
# Cannot Compare to One Who Retreats
## 萬事無如退步人

Undergoing ten thousand things[1] cannot compare      1
    to one who retreats.
The body free as a solitary cloud or a roaming crane;
Palm tree arches stretch for ten miles, I come and go.
With a laugh I bow to the full moon perched atop
    a mountain peak.

Undergoing ten thousand things cannot compare to      5
    resting from retreating.
Inherently there is no realization or cultivation,
The moon hangs high through a clear window.
The tended chrysanthemums bloom in the fall.

Undergoing ten thousand things cannot compare to
    sleeping through retreating.
I dimly know the teachings, but I am at ease.      10
A lacquer tree's usefulness causes people to cut it,
While oil can illumine the darkness, burning all night long.

---

1. 萬事: All the various activities of life.

# MASTER FODENG SHOUXUN

**Master Fodeng Shouxun** (1079-1134) was a monastic from Zhejiang Province. He ordained in the Linji Chan School under **Master Fojian Huiqian**. Later, he established Yizhong Temple on Mount He, and as such is sometimes known as "Heshan Shouxun."

His poem, "Watching the Sky All Day without Lifting One's Head" is collected in the *Record of the Jiatai Era's Transmission of the Lamp.*

佛

燈

守

珣

# Watching the Sky All Day
## without Lifting One's Head
終日看天不舉頭

Watching the sky all day without lifting one's head,
As the peach blossoms reach their most beautiful,
    you raise your gaze.
Even if there were a net across the heavens,
Go through the mind's impenetrable barrier and one can rest.

# MASTER XUEDOU CHONGXIAN

**Master Xuedou Chongxian** (980-1052) was a monastic from Sichuan Province. He was ordained in the Yunmen Chan School under **Master Zhimen Guangzuo**. He was referred to posthumously as **Mingjue**, "Bright Enlightenment," and his collected works are contained within the text *Sayings of Chan Master Mingjue*.

Xuedou Chongxian's poetry also accompanies the *gongans* contained in the *Blue Cliff Record*. His poem "Old Juzhi Loved to Teach with One Finger" is included in the collection.

# Old Juzhi Loved to Teach with One Finger
## 對揚深愛老俱胝

Old Juzhi loved to teach with one finger.[1]
Is there anything in the universe but emptiness?
Once, he threw a piece of driftwood into the great ocean,
In the darkness the waves carried it to a blind seaturtle.

---

1. 對揚: In this instance, a reference to Master Juzhi Yizhi, who taught by silently holding up his finger. A popular *gongan* recounts how he cut off the finger of a boy who attempted to imitate him without knowing the significance of his gesture. After the boy realized his error he attained enlightenment.

# MASTER TONGAN CHANGCHA

**Master Tongan Changcha** was a monastic and a student of **Master Jiufeng Daoqian**. He taught at Tongan Monastery on Mount Fengqi.

One of his major works, *Chan Master Tongan Changcha Discusses the Ten Philosophical Ideas,* survives today.

# Encouraging Cultivation
勸修行

Coming into the world covered with fur and sporting horns,
The blue lotus blossoms in fire.
Amid the sea of affliction, take it as a sprinkling of dew;
Be the thunder cloud that breaks the mountain of ignorance.

# MASTER CHALINGYU

茶陵郁

**Master Chalingyu** was an eleventh century monastic. He was not widely traveled or particularly well-known, and is most remembered as an early teacher of **Master Baiyun Shouduan**.

His poem "I Have a Single Bright Pearl" is collected in the *Origins of the Transmission of the Five Schools.*

# I Have a Single Bright Pearl
## 我有明珠一顆

I have a single bright pearl,
Long imprisoned in dust.
Now that the dust is gone, brightness shines through
Illuminating all mountains and rivers.

# MASTER WUZHUO MIAOZONG

**Master Wuzhuo Miaozong** was a twelfth century female monastic from Jiangsu Province. It is said that she once attended a lecture by **Master Dahui Zonggao** in which he scolded all in attendance. Everyone in the audience was shocked, except for Wuzhuo Miaozong who was gladdened by Dahui Zonggao's oratory. She approached him and requested a Dharma name, to which Dahui Zonggao gave her the name Wuzhuo, "non-attachment."

Her poem "A Slip of a Boat on Boundless Waters" is collected in the *Record of the Jiatai Era's Transmission of the Lamp.*

# A Slip of a Boat on Boundless Waters
## 一葉扁舟泛渺茫

A slip of a boat on boundless waters,
With oar and paddle, escapes from music and sound.
Clouds, mountains, seas, and the moon are all discarded—
Then win Zhuang Zhou's long dream of the butterfly.[1]

---

1. 蝶夢長: Reference to the Chinese philosopher Zhuangzi. In chapter 2 of the eponymous *Zhuangzi*, he recounts having a dream of life as a butterfly. After awakening he is unable to distinguish if he dreamt of life as a butterfly, or if he was truly a butterfly and was now dreaming of life as Zhuangzi.

# Master Kuoan Shiyuan

**Master Kuoan Shiyuan** was a twelfth century monastic most popularly known for his work "Poems on the Ten Ox-Herding Pictures." The images, each accompanied by a short poem, depict the stages of spiritual development by using an ox as an extended metaphor for the practitioner's mastery of the mind.

The tradition of depicting the unruly nature of the mind as an ox stretches back to the Buddha, and while there were likely other sets of ox pictures and poems, Kuoan Shiyuan's have become the most copied and prominent.

# Poems on the Ten Ox-Herding Pictures
## 十牛圖頌

**I. Searching for the Ox**                                          1
Hurriedly parting the brush searching for it
Water wide, mountains far away, road long;
Tired and exhausted, still it eludes me.
The chirr of evening cicadas in the maple trees              5
    is all that is heard.

**II. Spotting the Ox's Tracks**
Its tracks can be seen under the trees along the river,
Parting the brush, do you see it?
Even in such a remote place deep in the mountains,
How can the vast sky hide its nose?                            10

**III. Seeing the Ox**
An oriole calls from a green bough—
Warm sun, gentle breeze, willow-lined river;
No place left to hide
Its head and horns, there, real to life.                       15

**IV. Capturing the Ox**
With all my effort, I take hold of it;
Strong and stubborn, it is hard to control.
One minute it is on the high plateau,
The next in a place deep among the clouds.                    20

### V. Herding the Ox

Never be without whip and tether
Or it might stray in the world.
Herded properly it will become tame,
25   Untethered it will follow unforced.

### VI. Riding the Ox Home

Riding the ox, meandering homeward;
Seeing off the evening clouds, playing a flute,
Clapping and singing so happily—
30   Knowing well, why speak of it?

### VII. Ox Forgotten, the Man Remains

Having ridden home on the ox
Both man and ox are free.
Though the sun is high, still the man seems to dream;
35   Whip and tether lie unused in his thatched hut.

### VIII. Man and Ox Both Forgotten

Whip and tether, man and ox all empty;
The vast blue sky difficult to fathom.
How can a snowflake survive inside a fiery stove?
40   Now I join the enlightened ones of the past.

### IX. Returning to the Source and Origin

It is a struggle to return to the source and origin,
Nothing surpasses this. Without sight or sound,
Unable to see the tree from the woods;
45   The water vast, the flowers red because it is so.

**X. Entering the World, Hands Free**
Barechested and barefoot entering the world
Covered with dust and ashes, smiling broadly;
There's no need for magic spells
To make the barren branch bloom.                    50

# ZHU DUNRU

**Zhu Dunru** (1081-1159), also known by the pen-name **Yanhuo**, was a poet from Henan Province. His works include *Poems and Writings of Old Man Yanhuo* and *Songs of the Woodcutter*.

# Worldly Affairs Are Short as a Spring Dream
*Tune: West River Moon*

世事短如春夢

Worldly affairs are short as a spring dream;                    1
Human sentiment is as thin as autumn clouds.
There is no need to compare and allow hardships to
    belabor the mind;
All things have their destinies.

Luckily, I have three cups of good wine                         5
And have met a new blossom.
Joyful and laughing for a time when we come together;
Whether tomorrow is bright or cloudy is uncertain.

# LI QINGZHAO

李清照

**Li Qingzhao** (b. 1084) was a female writer and poet from Shandong Province. She is widely regarded as China's greatest female poet, and her work is sonorous, delightful, and refreshing.

When the Jin armies invaded the Song capital of Kaifeng, the fighting reached Li Qingzhao's residence and her home was burned to the ground. Her husband died while traveling south with the rest of the Song court, and the loss greatly impacted her and her work.

Li Qingzhao's extant poetry is largely collected in the *Lyrics of Shuyu*.

# The Revelry Has Ended, Fragrance Washed Away

*Tune: The Spring of Wuling*

風住塵香花已盡

The revelry has ended, fragrance washed away;        1
    fallen flowers scattered on the ground.
It is late, I've grown too tired to comb my hair.
The place remains, the people are different; all has changed.
I wish to speak, but tears fall instead.

I hear at Twin Creeks[1] it is still spring;        5
How I'd love to drift there in a boat.
My only fear is that such a small boat
Could not carry so much grief.

---

1. 雙溪: Located in Zhejiang Province.

# XIN QIJI

**Xin Qiji** (1140-1207), also known by the penname **Jiaxuan**, was a soldier, poet, and government official from Shandong Province. Born after the Jin invasion, he spent his youth in military service leading skirmishes to the north. His heroism earned him a post in the Southern Song government after open hostilities ended.

His poetry is noted for its boldness and displays of patriotic fervor. A collection of his poetry, *Lyrics of Jiaxuan*, contains over six hundred poems.

辛棄疾

# Green Mountains Enjoy Talking with Noblemen
### Tune: Kindhearted Barbarian
青山欲共高人語

*Written for Chancellor Ye at Shangxin Pavilion in Jinling.*

Green mountains enjoy talking with noblemen.                    1
Hurried as ten thousand horses, passing uncountably,
Stationary as the misty rain,
Hoping one comes. In the end, no one comes.

People talk about my hair;                                       5
It always seems to grow whiter when I'm sad.
I clap my hands and laugh at a gull—
My whole body is nothing but sadness.

# Night Walk on Yellow Sand Road

*Tune: West River Moon*

夜行黄沙道中

1  The bright moon hangs on a branch, startled by a magpie;
    At midnight a cicada cries in a fresh breeze.
    The fragrance of rice tells of a bumper harvest;
    The frogs are heard croaking all about.

5  Seven or eight stars hanging in the sky,
    Two or three drops of rain before the mountain.
    An old inn stands beside the forest near the shrine;
    At a turn in the road, a bridge suddenly comes into view.

# When I Was Young, I Never Tasted Worry

*Tune: The Ugly Slave*

少年不識愁滋味

*Written on the wall along the path to Mount Bo.*

When I was young, I never tasted worry,                           1
I loved to climb the storied tower.

I loved to climb the storied tower,
Composing new poems, I was forced to speak of worries.

And now I fully know worries,                                     5
I wish to speak, but cannot.

I wish to speak, but cannot,
I just say, "It is brisk. What a wonderful autumn."

# Too Much! I'm Getting Old!

### Tune: Feasting the Bridegroom

甚矣吾衰矣

*At the Pavilion of Yizhong Garden, your servant wrote this poem. One day, as I sat alone at Tingyun, the water murmured and the mountain colored, competing with one another to entertain. Mount Yixi wanted to invoke a precedent, so as a result I wrote some words to imitate Yuanmin when he thought of his relatives and friends.*

1　Too much! I'm getting old!
　I am disappointed that my friends are dwindling;
　How many are left now?

　My white hair—three thousand strands—hangs in vain,
5　I laugh at the ten thousand events of the human world.

　May I ask what can make you happy?
　I see the green mountains, how beautiful they are,
　And expect the green mountains see me this way too.

　Our feelings and features are almost the same,
10　An old man scratching his head in the east window.

Thinking of Yuanmin,[1] I finish a poem at Tingyun
With a savor of the times.
How people so sought fame around the Yangzi River beyond
    Fuhu and Nanjing.

Know the wonders of undecanted wine!
I turned my head to call the clouds to fly and the winds to race.    15

I don't hate the ancients I never saw, I hate the ancients
Who never saw my wildness!
Only two or three ever understood me.

---

1. 陶淵明: Tao Yuanmin, fifth century pastoral poet.

# Lu You

**Lu You** (1125-1210), also known by the penname **Fangwong**, was a poet, scholar, and government official. He was born after the Jin invasion, and grew up very invested in politics and the welfare of the people.

Lu You was a prolific writer, and over nine thousand of his poems have survived, collected in various texts such as the *Poetry Manuscript of Jiannan*, *Writings from Weinan*, and *Lyrics of Fangwong*. His work is bold and unrelenting, and many of his compositions express his hopes for a reunified China.

# To Show My Sons
## 示兒

As I die, I know all things are empty,
Still, I am sad that I never saw the nation unified.[1]
The day the emperor's troops march north to retake the country
Don't forget to tell your father at the family memorial.

---

1. Near the end of Lu You's life the Song dynasty had still retreated to the south, and the Mongols were waging war against the Jin state. The Song dynasty would never again control a unified China.

# Dream Record Sent to Shi Bohun[1]
## *Tune: Night Revels in the Palace*
記夢寄師伯渾

1  A snowy morning, the sound of a wavering flute arises;
Like traveling somewhere in a dream,
I know not where this is.
Armored cavalry, silent, appear as water.

5  Thinking of the borderlands,
West of Yanmen,
Near Qinghai.[2]

Sleeping in the cold under a lamp,
The water clock has stopped.
10  The moon askew through a paper window,
I appoint myself as lord
    over these tens of thousands of miles.

Who would know?
Though I am graying at the temples,
My mind has not died.

---

1. 師伯渾: A friend of Lu You.
2. This describes the Southern Song dynasty's northern border.

# Zhang Jiucheng

**Zhang Jiucheng** (1092-1159), also known as **Layman Hengpu**, was a government official and devout lay Buddhist follower. He was a student of **Master Dahui Zonggao**.

He passed the imperial examination following the Jin invasion, and was one of the officials to speak out against **Chancellor Qin Kuai**, who is now remembered as a schemer and a traitor. For his dissidence he was exiled far away from the capital to Nanan in Fujian Province.

His poem "The Spring Moon at Night—a Frog Croaks" is collected in the *Record of the Jiatai Era's Transmission of the Lamp*. The majority of his work is compiled in the *Hengpu Collection*.

## The Spring Moon at Night—a Frog Croaks
### 春天月夜一聲蛙

The spring moon at night—a frog croaks;
Heaven and earth break and become one.
At this time, who will understand?
Atop the peak, one's feet hurt from the sand.

# ZHU XI

**Zhu Xi** (1130-1200) was a Confucian scholar, rationalist philosopher, and government official. Though his academic work was based on Confucian texts, his thought was heavily influenced by Buddhism. He was well versed in the sutras and studied the works of **Master Dahui Zonggao**, **Master Gueishan Lingyou**, and **Master Yongming Yanshou**. He is also said to have practiced meditation.

In his later years he built himself a thatched hut on Mount Yungu and lived in seclusion.

# Thoughts on Reading
## 觀書有感

A half acre square pond, like a mirror;
Light from the heavens, and the shadows of the clouds,
    together come and go.
How can a stream be as clear as this?
Because its original source comes from rushing water.

# Zhang Xiaoxiang

**Zhang Xiaoxiang** (1132-1169) was a poet from Anhui Province. He also went by the name **Yuhu Jushi**, "layman of the lake." His surviving poetry collections include *Water Songs* and *Songs from the Six Provinces*.

張

孝

祥

# Passing Dongting
*Tune: The Charm of Niannu*
過洞庭

1  Dongting Lake, Qingcao Lake,[1]
Near mid-autumn.
Calm; no winds blow.

Thirty thousand acres shimmer with a jade glow,
5  Carrying my leaflike boat.

The pure moon shines upon it,
The Milky Way casts a shadow.
It is clear and bright inside and out.

With joy, my mind understands,
10  But this wondrous place is difficult to speak of.

I should remember my years in seas of Linghai,[2]
Illuminating myself with solitary light,
My organs like snow and ice.

Hair sparse, clothing thin and cold;
15  Steadily my boat proceeds
      between the vast sky and the water.

---

1. 洞庭青草: Lakes located in Hunan Province.
2. 嶺海: Collective name for the mountainous regions of southern China.

The Xijiang[1] overflows—
Lean on the Big Dipper.
All things are my guests.

Tying the ship off, I laugh,
What night is it tonight?                                    20

---

1. 西江: Tributary of the Pearl River that flows south of Hunan Province.

# LUO DAJING

**Luo Dajing** (1196~1252) was a poet and government official from Jiangxi Province. After serving as a low level administrator for a time, Luo Dajing was removed from his post due to infighting amongst the officials.

His greatest work, *Crane Forest, Jade Dew* is critical of government and shows Luo Dajing's great empathy for the common people.

# The Way Is Not in Language
## 道不在語言文字

The painter of snow                                                    1
    cannot capture the purity of snow.
The painter of the moon
    cannot capture the brightness of the moon.
The painter of the flower
    cannot capture the fragrance of the flower.
The painter of a spring
    cannot capture the murmur of the spring.
The painter of a figure                                               5
    cannot capture the emotions of the figure.
Naturally, language
    cannot fully convey the Way.

# WU WENYING

**Wu Wenying** (1200-1260), also known by the penname **Mengchuang**, was a poet from Zhejiang Province. His poetry was considered craftsmen-like and orthodox by his contemporaries. His work is compiled in the four-volume *Lyrics of Mengchuang*.

# Where Has the Character for "Worries" Come From?

*Tune: Tang Ditty*

何處合成愁

Where has the character for "worries" (愁) come from?　　　　1
Those departing have the mind (心) of autumn (秋).[1]

Though it does not rain,
　　one hears the wind through the plantains.
They all say that the nights are cool,
　　and the weather is fine.

The moon is bright,　　　　　　　　　　　　　　　　　5
But I fear ascending the tower.

In my dreams, the years and happenings stop,
There are no flowers, the misty river flows.

The swallows bid adieu,
But the guest remains.[2]　　　　　　　　　　　　　　　10

The weeping willows have not encircled and held him fast,
Still, long, long,
Has the boat remained docked.

---

1. This is a reference to the composition of the Chinese character. "Worry" is made up of the components for "autumn" and "mind."

2. 客: The author referring to himself. He is a "guest" and not a host because he is far from his homeland.

# WEN TIANXIANG

**Wen Tianxiang** (1236-1283) was a government official, military leader, and poet from Jiangxi Province. Having passed the imperial examination at a young age, he gradually rose up the ranks and was serving as chancellor during the Jin invasion.

Wen Tianxiang was offered a position in the Jin government, but he refused to betray the Song dynasty emperor. After the Song court moved south he continued to resist, and was captured. He was tortured for years and ultimately executed, never wavering in his loyalties.

Wen Tianxiang's patriotic poetry became well known during his own lifetime, particularly his *Song of Righteousness*, which he wrote leading up to his execution. The selected poem, "Crossing Lingding Sea," contains Wen Tianxiang's two most famous lines, which close the poem: "Since the beginning, who has not died? / Let me leave a loyal heart shinning in history."

# Crossing Lingding Sea
## 過零丁洋

I recall the hardships and difficult times 1
    from my early years;
The fighting, though sparse,
    has gone on for four astrological cycles.[1]
The mountains and rivers are broken into pieces
    and blown away by the wind;
The body is carried as the rain carries duckweed.

The Huangkong shores bespeak fear, 5
The Lingding Sea sighs with loneliness.
Since the beginning, who has not died?
Let me leave a loyal heart shinning in history.

---

1. 四周星: Forty-eight years, corresponding to four cycles of the twelve
sign Chinese zodiac.

# JIANG JIE

**Jiang Jie** (1245~1301), also known by the penname **Zhushan**, was a poet from Jiangsu Province. His writing is philosophical, rhythmic, and refreshing. His subjects often include reminiscence and nostalgia for the past.

His works include *A Detailed Analysis of Literature* and the *Lyrics of Zhushan.*

# Crossing Wujiang[1] by Boat
### Tune: A Sprig of Plum
### 舟過吳江

My spring worries wait for the wine to run out;                1
The boat rocks on the river,
A tavern flag beckons.

Qiuliang crossing and Tailiang bridge;[2]
Again the wind blows and blows,                                5
Again the rain falls and falls.

When can I go home to wash my traveler's robe?
The flute, with silver inscription, plays;
Incense, like the heart, burns.

Time all too easily deserts a man.                             10
The cherries redden,
The plantains become greener.

---

1. 吳江: District in Jiangsu Province.
2. 秋娘渡 泰娘橋: Two famous sites in Wujiang. They are named for prominent Tang dynasty singers.

# Listening to the Falling Rain

*Tune: The Beautiful Lady Yu*

聽雨

1  In the pleasure houses of my youth, I listened to the rain;
Red candles glowing faintly beside the curtained bed.

In my middle years, I listened to the rain while
     traveling by boat,
The vast river under low clouds,
5  A lone crane calling the west wind.

Today, living in a monastery, I listen to the rain,
My temples speckled white.

Joy and sadness, meeting and parting—these have
     nothing to do with us.
Let it rain upon the steps
10  And drip until the break of day.

# IV

1271–1368

# Yuan Dynasty

# YELü CHUCAI

**Yelü Chucai** (1190-1244), also known by the Dharma name **Zhanran**, was a poet, government official, and chancellor to Ghenghis Khan. A devout Khitanese Buddhist, Yelu Chucai petitioned the Mongols to curb their violence as they overtook the Jin dynasty. On multiple occasions he was able to convince the Mongol military to govern and tax a conquered region, rather than slaughter its inhabitants.

His poetry is collected in the *Works of Layman Zhanran*.

## Epiphany from Cultivation
修行一得

Marching for ten thousand miles through
    wind-blown sand—
North, south, east, and west, it's all home.
In the end, the heart is emptied,
Nothing stirs; the mind a white lotus.

# MASTER SHIWU QINGGONG

**Master Shiwu Qinggong** (1272-1352) was a monastic of the Caodong Chan School. He lived most of his life as a mountain hermit, and the scenery of the mountains dominates much of his work.

The calligraphy selection is by twentieth century Taiwanese calligrapher and painter **Xie Zhiliu**.

# Sewing Poem
## 裁縫詩

Going everywhere with scissors and measuring stick,
The thread goes, the needle comes; busy every day.
Having measured everyone's long and short[1]
When will I measure my own long and short?

---

1. 長短: Metaphor for good and bad qualities.

# Wu Cheng

**Wu Cheng** (1249–1333) was a scholar and historian from Jiangxi Province. He was a college professor and authored a biography of **Emperor Yingzong,** in addition to several commentaries on the Confucian Classics.

# On the Hall of Benevolence and Longevity
## 仁壽堂說

The benevolent enjoy long life. All things created by heaven and earth have the mind of benevolence. Heaven and earth have the greatest longevity. The benevolence of the sage is like heaven and earth, so the life of the sage is the longest.

Possessing complete virtue is naturally not easy. [Consider] the three hundred forms of etiquette, or the three thousand dignified manners, not one among them lacks benevolence. Practicing just one could be called benevolence, and allow one to enjoy a long life. Adhering to this, I often observe all walks of life in the world. He who is gentle, kind, tolerant, honest, or sincere will enjoy a long life, for gentleness, kindness, tolerance, honesty, and sincerity are each a part of benevolence. Old Man Du of Heyang is eighty-two. He is considered a good man throughout the whole village and named his dwelling the Hall of Benevolence and Longevity. I never met the old man, but I know that he must be a gentle, kind, tolerant, honest and sincere person. Anyone who possesses even one of the five virtues ought to enjoy long life, not to mention possessing two, three, four or five virtues!

This autumn, while in the capital, I met his son and was able to see the record of the Hall of Benevolence and Longevity written by such a great scholar of our times. For this reason, I say and promote the idea that the benevolent enjoy long life.

梵
琦
楚
石

# MASTER FANQI CHUSHI

**Master Fanqi Chushi** (1296-1370) was a monastic from Zhejiang Province. He ordained at a young age in the Linji Chan School and was honored by emperors of both the Yuan and Ming dynasties as the preeminent monastic of the day.

Late in life he built a hermitage he called "Xizhai" and focused his effort on Pure Land practice. It was during this time that he wrote the *Xizhai Pure Land Poems*. The collection features breathtaking descriptions of the Pure Land and hums with devotion for Amitabha Buddha, while also featuring the more earthly and practical qualities endemic of the Chan School. Fanqi Chushi depicts the popular elements of the Pure Land aesthetic, while spurring on the reader to urgently cultivate.

Selections from the *Xizhai Pure Land Poems* are given here, with each numbered for its place in the complete collection.

# Xizhai Pure Land Poems
## (selections)
### 西齋淨土詩

**[5]**

Overlooking the Golden Lotus Treasure Realm;[1]
    how far away,
Terraces, one by one, reach to the sky.
Orioles sing beautifully in perpetual spring;
The tender limbs of jade trees never wither.
The sound of flowing water turns and follows each riverbend,
Innumerable wonderful flowers fall in the breeze.
Feral people, you choose which day you will return,[2]
Why wait for the sages to summon you?

**[8]**

Let go of body and mind and the Buddha appears
    before you,
One's ears are always filled with the sound of the
    Dharma proclaimed.
The wind through the tree branches plays the song of the
    unborn—
Contemplate the sun; always shining, never night.
Walking on steps of jade, clouds rise gradually;
Sitting under trees of pearl, the moon is so beautiful.
Ordinary beings arrive here and all become saints,
With no need to spend *kalpas* to attain Buddhahood.

---

1. 金蓮寶界: Synonym of Amitabha's Pure Land.
2. Being reborn in the Pure Land is commonly called "returning" to the Pure Land.

**[11]**

Though created in paintings, wood carvings, and clay statues,
The true Buddha is already very clear.
Taking refuge is not others' family affairs;
Merit and virtue come from oneself.
The ten thousand trees and the flower blossoms bloom,
    for the earth is warm.
The moon is reflected in one thousand rivers,
    for the water is clear.
Every morning and evening, paying homage,
There all may enter the city of ultimate bliss.[1]

**[12]**

Master reciting the Buddha's name and
    unwholesomeness erases itself:
One returns and resides in the Pure Land of Ultimate Bliss.
The grass and trees in the monastery are beautiful,
The mountains and rivers of this great land are splendid.
One then steps into the realm of fragrance,
Flower buds blossom into precious lotuses on their own,[2]
All have a brilliant shining halo and golden complexion.
Heaven and the human realm cannot compare.

**[13]**

No heavenly being has not realized supernatural powers,
Each gold colored and alike,
Scattering many kinds of wondrous flowers as Buddhist practice;

---

1. 極樂城: Synonym of Amitabha's Pure Land.
2. Beings reborn in the Pure Land and said to be born from lotus blossoms rather than wombs.

As the unwholesomeness of afflictions end,
    a fragrant wind arises.
Light from their bodies contacts and softens one's essence.
The sound of their music emanates and speaks of
    suffering and emptiness.
But, leaning against carved railings,
    they watch the jeweled trees,
Infinite Buddha lands within.

**[17]**
Truly, there is no death in the Pure Land.
In the shade of the clouds, watching the sun set—
Pearl towers, jade shrines, constructed in the sky,
The green trees and golden flowers concealing one's practice.
Gust after gust of good winds blow the lotuses in waves,
Trickling, trickling streams in which Mandarin ducks swim.
Those who now recall the song of the unborn,
Together with others who know it well, harmonize as one.

**[19]**
Many times I dream I have arrived at the home
    of the Dharma king.
Coming or going, the road is clear, I do not falter,
From the water arise pearl banners like the sun and moon,
The sky is lined with jeweled umbrella clouds.
Mandarin ducks face one another and bathe in golden ponds,
Pairs of parrots hold flowers from the jade trees in their beaks.
I sleep well, not realizing who has awoken me.
Smoke scatters from the censer in the slanted rays
    of the setting sun.

**[21]**

Pointing far off to my home[1] where the sun sets,
One road returns there, straight as a string.
In the sky many kinds of music play;
On the water many lotuses bloom.
The branches and twigs of many trees become hundreds
    of treasures.
Living together, our lives and food and drink exceed that
    of heavenly beings.
My teacher has made vows[2] we should all undertake,
To not waste fifty years of diligence.

**[22]**

One lotus, one sage contained,
One life of perfect virtue, one flower blooms.[3]
With a thought, necklaces of precious stones adorn the body,
With a thought, any bowl fills with ghee.
The golden shrine shines, swallowing the sun and moon;
Jade towers, with no place for dust to fall.
The Dharma king speaks the truth to me,
Until the universe fills with smiles.

**[23]**

Shrines of the greatest pearl and groves of jade—
Wherever one sits, or lies down,

---

1. 家鄉: The Pure Land is commonly referred to as one's home.

2. 吾師有願: Reference to Amitabha Buddha's forty-eight vows.

3. Though beings born into the Pure Land arrive inside lotus blossoms, the lotus does not bloom until the practitioner has attained a certain degree of practice.

or walks in meditation the ground is golden.
The *sarika* birds,[1] again and again, sing wondrous songs,
The *kalavinka* birds,[2] so, so clear, perform the Buddha's song.
Return to listen and suddenly awaken to the unborn,
Living in such surroundings, the mind ever unmoving.
All that one sees is the Pure Land,
Coming from many *kalpas* past to now.

## [24]
The causes and conditions for the Pure Land
    have already been created.
All time appears before me as a day:
In late afternoon I strive to be more wholesome,
Following the day under the vast sky.
The Tathagata himself touches my head with his
    precious hands,[3]
Bodhisattvas pat my shoulder with their golden bodies.
I will not rely on a placenta to be born into some illusive body,
My home already has a lotus in a jade pond.

## [29]
This land's purity allows people to attain Buddhahood.
The nature of the Saha World will change at once:
Like a fish escaping from fine netting into the great sea,
Or a swallow avoiding an arrow
    and flying far off in the sky.

---

1. 舍利: Mythic birds said to inhabit the Pure Land.
2. 頻伽: Mythic birds said to inhabit the Pure Land.
3. Reference to Amitabha Buddha appearing before a Pure Land practitioner at the moment of death.

The coming and going of rebirth stops now.
The afflictions of birth and death can no longer bind,
"No mind" is real, pure, and tranquil,
When attached to impurity, how can one look upon
    the treasured lotus?

[31]

Palaces of gold and silver float atop colored clouds,
Those who recite the Buddha's name reside there and gaze afar:
Jeweled trees of many colors grow together,
Divine birds sing a thousand songs in harmony,
Crystal bowls fill with ghee on their own,
Green plates are ever filled with honey dew.
Unlike the Himalayas, which grow many medicinal herbs,
But those sentient beings without merit taste them as sour.

[32]

Do not go to the Saha World—
One should be reborn in the Land of Ultimate Bliss.
Without mastering reciting the Buddha's name,
How can you transcend ordinary beings and fulfill
    your powerful vows?
A fragrant mist fills the sky, enveloping like a shadow,
A warm breeze blows through the trees and becomes music.
Clearly understand the meaning of suchness
And be able to see one's *mani* pearl as crystal.

[33]

The Buddha taught in the Saha World—
But how evil sentient beings are!

Wishing to reveal the secret of *nirvana*,
He had to point towards Amitabha in the Pure Land.[1]
White clouds half conceal green mountains;
In the beginning, the red sun rises from the blue ocean waves.
Traversing for countless *kalpas* without enlightenment,
From east to west, who can say they are not mistaken?

[36]
Day and night one thinks of returning, but cannot,
In a dream this traveler's soul flies back,
Awake now, what has happened to the sound of the swallows?
Watching, waiting for letters from home; few to none.
Many times watching the low-slung moon
A life of leaning against the railing, watching remnants
        of the sunset.
A lotus pad, large as a boat, within a golden pond
Wishing to see tens of blossoms enveloping.

[37]
I once heard that the crane is a divine bird,
Every day it flies here to sing its good song,
I wish to send a letter to all good Dharma friends,
For they should know my life's intent.
Having longed for the Pure Land, finally I return,
Visited from far away, willfully held in a lotus.
One hundred years pass like a snap of the fingers,
Only fear the Saha World's deep connections.

---

1. Reference to the *Amitabha Sutra*, where Sakyamuni Buddha tells the
assembly of Amitabha Buddha.

**[38]**

A bit of time for a bit of gold.
I implore you: recite the Buddha's name,
    resolve to return early on
And directly get to live in the precious palace.
Avoid shriveled skin and white hair.
Incense smoke still billows from the censer,
The Dharma vessel[1] waits in the sky, here from far away.
Though temples in the world may be pure,
It is only Amitabha's vow that is profound.

**[40]**

Do not be too quick to say you will return home late,
There is no need for you to speak, for I already know.
The road we travel is uneven, nothing good about it.
Sorry for life, for we do not live long,
Sorry for this aged face, seen clearly in the mirror,
Sorry for the few black hairs, the others long and white.
Reading Nanping's *Ultimate Bliss Rhapsody*[2]
Upon the roof, watching the descending moon's
    grateful charm.

**[46]**

"The mind is the Buddha," cuts off thousands of differences,
The teachings and Chan are of one family.
Enlightenment, with its infinite good physical marks;
Such light pouring forth cannot be spoken of as river sand.

---

1. 法駕: A being that embodies the Dharma. Here it refers to Amitabha.
2 安養賦: Pure Land treatise composed by Master Zhijue Yanshou at Mount Nanping.

Other places cannot compare to its wondrous beauty,
How can the depth of the original vow[1] be overstated?
Most of one's practice should occur early on,
Such that, at death, one avoids the
    obstructions of karmic connections.

## [58]

Ten billion *kalpas* of unwholesomeness
    lead to birth and death;
Simply recall Amitabha's name and it is all eliminated.
When deluded, illusory thoughts are as a spring dream;
The Buddha's true body is the same as the vast universe.
A crystal palace, encircled with one thousand pillars,
A grove of interwoven clouds
    where ten thousand flowers blossom,
The ignorant mind does not distinguish
    between high and low.
Ascend to the highest golden platform; then you can rest.

## [61]

The five kinds of chaos torture us,
    and the Way is not attained;
All sages make vows and do not take them lightly.
Inside every light is Amitabha's image.
In our dreams, Amitabha writes the name of
    universal wisdom.
Embroidering the Buddha's image and keeping a
    vegetarian diet, still one must prevent backsliding.

---

1. 本願: The vow to become a Buddha.

The procession is already here; hurry to catch it.
When faced with the wind,
    do not cry the red willow's tears.
Just follow the road to the Western Pure Land, and go.


[62]
If the water is clear, it will reflect the moon,
The golden face of the Buddha statue
    appears in my mind.
A spring wind cannot revive dead branches;
A magnet has difficulty lifting a bent needle.
If one cannot be reborn in the Pure Land due to
    weighty karmic obstructions,
One should practice heartily to achieve success,
Such as one with the power of the
    nine crimson transmutations
Can point at iron and transform it to gold.


[65]
Every morning, every evening the Way is within the mind.
Every year conducting the same Buddhist services;
Advancing one's practice to reach the Pure Land.
All day paying homage to the Dharma king's palace—
One does not mind that incense darkens the monastic robes
And is not bothered when sweating hands
    turn the bowing mat red.
How many monastics are like this today
Who clearly know their master?

**[69]**

None of the thousands of sutras
  and tens of thousands of treatises do not point
Altogether, only to the road west.
With every thought, clean the filth from the mind;
With every moment, protect the sprouts of the Way[1]
  from beings scorched.
Dwelling on the lotus, tranquilly awaken; the body is
  safe and at peace.
Attain the fruit as thunder roars and the earth quakes,
It is a waste of effort to count the years;
A great *kalpa* in the Saha World is only suffering.

**[76]**

Looking west at red clouds and the white orb of the sun;
Looking up at the jewel throne and rose-gold body:
When one place is pure, all become pure.
If the mind has ten true thoughts, then all thoughts are true;
Those reborn in the city of ultimate bliss never return.
To the ends of this vast universe there is no more dust.
Having drifted all this way on the sea of suffering,
How fortunate to now be a person on the other shore.

**[77]**

So ignorant are those born in the Saha World,
They are bound by all this suffering, yet do not
  seek liberation,

---

1. 道芽: Derivative of the metaphor of karma as seeds, "sprouts of the Way" are the noble virtues that manifest due to one's previous good deeds.

With no pure karma in life
How can they be liberated in death?
Though encouraged by one hundred thousand sutras,
In a trillion people, only one or two will understand.
This precious, great sage, with golden arms,
Has come early to carry me into the lotus pond.

# V

1368–1644

# Ming Dynasty

# MASTER HANSHAN DEQING

**Master Hanshan Deqing** (1546-1623) was a monastic from Anhui Province. His uncle passed away when he was but seven years old, the loss made him realize the transitory nature of life and led him to a life of monasticism. His practice and teachings drew from both the Chan and Pure Land traditions. Over his lifetime Hanshan Deqing experienced periods of fame as well as slander, and the perpetual ebb and flow of life is a prominent subject of his writing.

Hanshan Deqing was a prolific writer, authoring poems, expositions of the Dharma, and commentaries on classical texts. His poem "Advice for the World," a selection from his popular *Collection of Old Man Hanshan's Dream Travels,* is typical of his down-to-earth teaching style. The essay "The Four Universal Vows" is an example of his exegetical work.

# Advice for the World
## 勸世詠

1 Red dust and white waves, vast and boundless;
Patience and gentleness are good ways.
Everywhere, following conditions as the years
    and months go on;
The time of one's whole life spent in contentment.

5 Do not let the mind be ignorant,
Never making the faults of others known.
Be prudent in dealing with others and do not regret;
Work patiently and be flexible.

The string of a rigid bow will always break first,
10 Every glance at a steel blade portends a wound.
A wagging tongue courts disaster,
A vicious heart is the cause of wrongdoing.

It is not necessary to argue if you or I are right or wrong,
Of what need is there to debate pro and con?
15 Since long ago, the world has had many shortcomings;
How can this illusory body be free of impermanence?

Losing once in a while will not hinder you,
There's no harm in giving in a little.
Only in spring are the willows green,
20 In the autumn breeze the chrysanthemums are yellow.

In the end, fame and glory are but a midnight dream,
Wealth and honor are just as autumn frost.
Old, sick, dead, born—who will take your place?
Everyone bears his sour, sweet, bitter, and hot.

Scheming people praise cleverness,                                    25
But heaven takes its time in its decisions.
Flattery, greed, and anger all lead to hell;
To be fair and upright is heaven.

The musk deer is killed because its musk is fragrant,
The more silk a silkworm spins the earlier it meets its end.      30
One dose of spiritual cultivation acts to settle the stomach;
Cups of peace and harmony are the two varieties of soup.

In life, the mind is vainly wasted on countless matters,
After death both hands are empty.
Joy and sorrow, parting and meeting happen every day;            35
Diligently pursue wealth and honor. Every day is busy.

Do not fight with others to prove your strength,
A hundred years is but a stage play.
The moment the drums and gongs go silent
You no longer know where your hometown is.                        40

# Four Vows
## 四願齊說

The four vows are: "Sentient beings are limitless, I vow to liberate them; afflictions are endless, I vow to eradicate them; teachings are infinite, I vow to learn them; Buddhahood is supreme, I vow to attain it." These four vows are the starting point for those who practice the way of the bodhisattva. A bodhisattva is not apart from people, but is an ordinary person with a great mind who lives in this world and has the will to seek out and attain Buddhahood. The teachings say that in order to attain the fruit of Buddahood, one must liberate sentient beings. To liberate sentient beings, one must first eradicate afflictions; to eradicate afflictions one must first learn all the teachings of the Buddha. This is how the four vows are established.

Sentient beings are the opposite of the Buddha. Affliction is the basis of sentient beings, and the teachings of the Buddha are the medicine with which to cure these afflictions. As sentient beings are limitless, so too are afflictions endless, and just as afflictions are endless so too are the teachings of the Buddha infinite. Those that are difficult to liberate, we vow to liberate. That which is difficult to eradicate, we vow to eradicate. That which is difficult to learn, we vow to learn. Having achieved these three things, even though Buddhahood is supreme, it can be attained. Thus they are called the four universal vows. One with a great mind is able to initiate such great vows, and one who has made such great vows has great deeds, great virtue, and great fame. All these vows are supported through great practice; they are not illusory vows. These four vows are not sought outside, but should be sought inside oneself.

Can this be clarified? Our minds are inherently Buddha, and sentient beings are by essence non-dualistic. With the cause of one thought of self, "self" is established, and that which is not myself is "other." The "other," with the addition of the "self," is a collection of beings that result in the creation of "sentient beings." Sentient beings have affliction as their basis, and the stronger the attachment to affliction, the firmer the sense of self becomes. With a solid sense of self, the other forms[1] will not perish. When "self" dies, "other" is not created. When "other" is not created, afflictions become empty. If the afflictions of my mind were eradicated, then I would be able to reflect back on "self" and "other" as sky flowers. Once the self is seen as a sky flower, one sees sentient beings as requesting a sky flower to bear fruit. When searching in such a way, how can anything be found?

With afflictions ended, sentient beings are empty. This is not liberation, yet the self is liberated; it is as if some form were present, though formless. Among all the people of the world, it cannot be that there is no self. There is "self," there is affliction. Using one's afflictions to deal with affairs is not the true mind. Affliction comes from affection. If one were to try to use the afflicted mind to eradicate affliction, it would be like attempting to hire a group of bandits to rob their own granaries. Using affection to end affection is like adding fire to fire; [both] will only grow and increase. Asking for desire to eradicate affliction is not possible. Thus you cannot neglect to learn the Buddha's teachings.

The Buddha's teachings go beyond affection and are an instrument for extinguishing afflictions. This is what is called "the teaching of emptiness." The teaching of emptiness is the Buddha's

---

1. Reference to the "four notions" of the *Diamond Sutra*: self, others, sentient beings, and longevity.

mind; seeing matters clearly is the Buddha's action. Those who study Buddhism use their minds to experience the Buddha's mind. In their daily affairs, they follow the Buddha's actions. This is attaining the Buddha mind within our minds; learning the Buddha's actions within our mind; eradicating the afflictions within our minds; and liberating the sentient beings within our minds. This is like using hot water to melt ice—excessive effort is not required.

Even though the four vows are not difficult, if we reflect upon them we can see that within the mind nothing is incomplete, and nothing needs to be borrowed from without. If we know that we need not seek outside, then all of us at that moment have a self in this body. Close to us are our families, siblings, wives, and slaves; more removed are the world, the country, people, animals, and sentient beings. If, in reflecting on our mind we use the afflicted mind to deal with our daily affairs then the six sense organs will be in conflict with each other; how then will our homes, nations, or the world be at peace? With the thought of using the teaching of emptiness to deal with one's daily affairs, each thought of affliction is transformed into wisdom's light and shines upon sentient beings—all will then return to intrinsic nature and be the same as the Buddha. With afflictions ended, sentient beings end. With the end of sentient beings, Buddhahood is attained. When people are my brothers and all things are equal then the vows will not have been in vain.

From this perspective, the supramundane teachings are achieved in this world. From this day forward everything we do, be it noble or common, must arise from the four universal vows; this is the Buddha's action. Are we to pursue vain activities for the sake of our senses or for the excitement? Having gained something from this, I now share it with you.

# MASTER ZIBO ZHENKE

**Master Zibo Zhenke** (1543-1603) was a monastic from Jiangsu Province. Though he was ordained in the Chan School, Zibo Zhenke was uniquely invested in Buddhist literature and textual criticism, and employed a teaching style that explicated sutras character by character. Believing that previously printed editions of the Buddhist canon were too difficult to read, he oversaw the creation of a new printed edition, called the *Fangce Canon*. This edition was based on the fifteenth century *Northern Canon* compared against the fourteenth century *Southern Canon* for textual accuracy.

Zibo Zhenke was also a staunch believer in monastic discipline, as evinced in his essay "On the Kitchen," which analyses the duties of the monastery cook in Buddhist doctrinal terms.

The calligraphy for Zibo Zhenke's poem "There Is Water in the Cauldron" is by contemporary scholar and calligrapher **Shen Peng**.

# On the Kitchen
## 示廚

The Buddha said, "The place in a temple for preparing offerings of food and drink for the Buddha, the Dharma, and the Sangha is known as the 'kitchen of accumulated fragrance.' But if those who prepare food and drink do not understand the three virtues or distinguish among the six flavors and if their three karmas of body, speech, and mind are impure, then the kitchen ought instead to be called the 'kitchen of accumulated filth.'"

What are the three virtues? They are purity, gentleness, and acting in accordance with the rule. What are the six flavors? They are plain, salty, spicy, sour, sweet, and bitter. If the food offered to the Buddha and the sangha is impure and consists of meat and fish, then the virtue of purity is lost; if it is not fine and pleasing and somewhat astringent, then the virtue of gentleness is lost; if it is not made on time, not properly made, not prepared carefully, and tasted before it is offered to the public, then the virtue of acting according to the rule is lost. If the three virtues are not blended in harmony with the six flavors, the three virtues are lost. The plain flavor is the essence of all flavors. The salty flavor is by nature moist, and it can moisten the muscles and skin. Thus, when blending flavors one should begin with salt. The spicy flavor is by nature hot, and can warm the coolness of the internal organs. Thus, the flavor of peppers is called "spicy." The sour flavor is by nature cooling and can release the ill effects of the other flavors. Thus the flavor of vinegar is called "sour." The sweet flavor is by nature gentle, and it can be gentle on the spleen and the stomach. Thus the flavor of sugar is called "sweet." The bitter flavor is by nature cold, and it is capable of releasing the heat of the internal organs. Thus acridity is called "bitter."

You people who examine and observe the three virtues and the six flavors, understanding how these virtues are virtues and how these flavors are flavors, in addition to holding no concept of self, others, sentient beings, or longevity,[1] do with your six sense organs and four limbs diligently and skillfully prepare food to offer to the Buddha and the sangha—such a person [gains] merit. It is as if one were to fill the vastness of space with the seven treasures[2] for endless kalpas, without giving rise to a single thought of stinginess or tiredness; the merit of [one who prepares food in this way] would be ten thousand times greater.

Any why is this? When the three virtues are not lacking and the six flavors are not absent, if such food and drink were smelled by the Buddha or entered the mouth of a monastic, it would be like smelling sandalwood and tasting sweet dew. The five internal organs[3] will be balanced and the skin smooth and pleasant, the body comfortable and the mind at peace, externally endowed with physical strength while internally endowed with mental vigor. Endowed with physical strength, the body is healthy. When the mind is endowed with vigor, the spirit will be undisturbed. When the body is healthy, one can advance towards the Way; when the spirit is undisturbed the wisdom of contemplation is easy to achieve. When food does not accord with the rule, then the body sickens and the mind is filled with anxieties. When body and mind are racked with illness and worry, it is impossible to progress toward enlightenment.

---

1. Reference to the "four notions" of the *Diamond Sutra*.

2. 七寶: Gold, silver, lapis lazuli, crystal, ruby, pearl, and carnelian. The act of filling space with these materials is a reference to the massive acts of generosity described in the *Diamond Sutra*.

3. 五內: Heart, lungs, liver, kidneys, and stomach.

This being the case, the lives and fates of those practicing the Way are inextricably linked to those in the kitchen. Therefore, cooks who do not distinguish among the three virtues and lack precision in the use of the six flavors are referred to as "ox-headed torturers from hell," or killers. If cooks distinguish among the three virtues, are precise in the six flavors, and prepare food and drink to offer to the Buddha and the sangha and by directing the six sense organs and the four limbs without a sense of self, others, sentient beings, or longevity, they are referred to as compassionate bodhisattvas. This is the reason for the expression: "The three thousand Buddhas were all produced in the kitchen."

If someone is always greedy and does not respect the virtuous and honorable, they will be reborn as a hungry ghost in hell. If someone is wasteful and does not consider future difficulties, they will be reborn in poverty. If someone who prepares food and drink and the six sense organs are uncontrolled, the nine orifices are unbridled,[1] the four limbs unclean, then they will be reborn as maggots and bedbugs.

All of the above is based on the Buddha's words. If someone hears or reads this they will develop a sense of shame. If a person practices it with a sense of respect, they will overcome ignorance while gaining wisdom, their wrongdoing will decrease as they accrue merit, and they will gain peace of mind and comfort. They will attain the supreme Way and become bodhisattvas. The Buddha's words are the truth. A child of the Buddha[2] in the kitchen will attain the Buddha-mind and be released from suffering.

---

1. 九竅: Both eyes, both ears, both nostrils, mouth, anus, and urinary tract.

2. 佛子: Monastic disciple of the Buddha.

# There Is Water in the Cauldron
## 水在釜中

There is water in the cauldron,
But without fire it cannot be heated.
There are seeds in the ground,
But without spring they won't sprout.
There is foolishness in the mind,
But it cannot be destroyed without study.

# MASTER LIANCHI ZHUHONG

**Master Lianchi Zhuhong** (1535-1615) was a monastic from Zhejiang Province. He was a practitioner of both Chan meditation and Pure Land recitation. He lived much of his life in an abandoned temple on Mount Yunqi, though he began to gather a large following based on the strength of his teaching and reputation for miracles. His teaching and writing, such as the poem "Seven Strokes Across," is accessible and impactful, and deals with day to day struggles rather than religious esoterica.

*Reverent Acts of the Monastics*, one of Lianchi Zhuhong's major works, collects and categorizes the stories of virtuous monastics from throughout Buddhist history. The work is far-reaching, though ten stories are selected here. Lianchi Zhuhong comments on several of the stories in the form of "praises," often addressing issues of his own time and decrying the decline of the sangha.

# Seven Strokes Across
## 七筆勾

**I.**

Parental kindness is weightier than the mountains,                    1
Five brazers of the three meats[1] are insufficient to repay it.
Only when his parents leave the world of defilement
Can a child become enlightened.
Alas, we arise in this world for a great matter,                    5
How can this be understood with common feelings?
Filial children and virtuous grandchildren,
It is good to study true emptiness.
This five-colored royal garment[2]—
    cross it out with a single stroke.

**II.**

The tender harmony of husband and wife,                    10
When will the ties of love and kindness end?
These ghosts cling to each other and pretend they live,
But when their karma expires they must part.
Alas, for your sentimental attachments
You put on chains and take up instruments of torture.                    15
See through this love
And each find a way out.
Husband and wife, as a fish is to water—
    cross them out with a single stroke.

---

1. 三牲: Beef, pork, and mutton. Commonly given as offerings in Chinese ancestor rites.
2. 五色金章: Cloak of the emperor. A symbol for fame and renown.

### III.

The body is like a sore or a wart;
20 Do not be worried for your children or grandchildren.
Recall Dou of Mount Yan,[1]
Does he still exist today?
Alas, everything comes to an end,
And with no children,
25 Who will be remembered?
It has always been so.
Children and grandchildren—
    cross them out with a single stroke.

### IV.

To come in first in the examination
Is said to be the time for a man's pride in his
    accomplishments.
30 The golden seal of office hangs like a star,
But power and influence don't last forever.
Alas, many things are vainly sought after.
The face of a child, with whitened hair,
Awakened from a dream to raw millet,[2]
35 Smiling at nothing.
Rank and reputation—
    cross them out with a single stroke.

---

1. 燕山竇: Dou's five children all passed the imperial examination and became government officials.

2. Reference to the Tang dynasty novel the Millet Dream, in which a man named Lusheng falls asleep and dreams of the events of the rest of his life. He awakens to find that the millet he began boiling before falling asleep is not yet cooked.

## V.

Wealth like that of the nobility,
You say it brings happiness, I say it brings anxiety.
Those who pursue it increase their suffering,
Those who have it worry they will lose it.                40
Alas, simple fare is better than delicacies;
A monk's robe is as good as embroidered garments.
Heaven and earth are home to me,
There is no need to make mansions.
Houses and land—                                          45
    cross them out with a single stroke.

## VI.

There is no end to study;
Attaining glory through artistry is like shooting
    at the Big Dipper.
Walking among the hundred arts with
A great capacity for wine and poetry.
Alas, dressed in beautiful garments,                      50
Of what is there to boast?
With birth and death in front of you,
At the moment it will scarcely save you,
Peerless writing—
    cross it out with a single stroke.

## VII.

Enjoying summer, going out in the spring;                 55
So many pleasures, singing and dancing.

Misty rain enchants the flowers and willows,[1]
Chess and wine delight relatives and friends.
Alas, on the heels of pleasure
60 Suffering follows
What a pity for the time wasted
A backward glance will show it was all for naught
Love and affection—
    cross them out with a single stroke.

---

1. 花柳: Symbols for feminine beauty.

# Reverent Acts of the Monastics
## (selections)
### 緇門崇行錄

## 1. The Hermit Zuoxi

Xuanlang of the Tang dynasty was a sixth-generation descendant of Fu Dashi. He was always complete in his ascetic practices, living among crags and beside gullies. He was also called Elder Zuoxi. He meditated in a single-room hut, but found it to be as vast as the dharma realm. He kept a single monastic robe for more than forty years, and used a single sitting mat for his whole life without changing it.

He did not seek out sutras, and would not burn a single candle lightly. He did not gaze upon [the Buddha's] sacred image, and did not walk a single false step. As he washed his bowl, monkeys would try to do so for him. As he recited the sutras, birds would flock together. Prefect Wang Zhengrong invited him to enter the city many times, but he was unwilling to go, and would give the excuse that he was ill.

*In Praise:*

People today have read Yongjia's letter to Xuanlang, and thus look down on his views, but they do not know what Yongjia was really criticizing.[1] His example is proper for us to learn from even today. Those with clear vision should understand this!

---

1. Yongjia Xuanjue, a contemporary of Zuoxi, wrote a letter criticizing his ascetic practices and imploring him to practice within the city. Zhuhong suggests that the criticism stems from being isolated from others, and thus not promoting Buddhism.

## 2. The Power to Protect the Main Shrine

Huizhu of the Tang dynasty was a man from Shizhou, Yonggui County. He was a master of vinaya studies and lived in Qinglin Temple. Once, a man named Linyang, who lacked faith, herded more than one hundred mules into the temple—throughout the main shrine, lecture hall, and monastic residences. No one dared to go against him. Huizhu returned from the village and saw the dirt and mess, then went to his quarters to get his staff and triple robe. He said to the mules with a sigh, "Today you live or die," and raised his staff against the mules. They soon fell to the ground like corpses, and he lifted them up and threw them in a pit. Shocked, the county magistrate apprehended the head of the temple and filed a complaint.

Lingyang happily said, "The vinaya master has destroyed my stinginess and greed; it has been a great benefit to me." He sent him ten *jin*[1] of aloe wood incense and ten bolts of silk. Later he returned to the capital and took the bodhisattva precepts from him.

## 3. Condemning Oneself and Receiving a Beating

Fayu of the Jin dynasty revered Daoan as his teacher. Later, he stayed at Changsha Temple in Jiangling, where he lectured on many sutras to over four hundred people. At one time, a monastic drank wine and was punished without being sent away. Daoan heard about the incident from afar, placed a thorny bramble cane in a bamboo tube, and sent it to Fayu.

As Yu opened it he saw the cane and said, "This must be because the monk drank wine. I have not taught you well, and have caused [my teacher] to worry from afar and send this gift to

---

1. 斤: Ancient Chinese unit of mass equal to roughly 500 grams.

me." Thus he banged the gong calling everyone to assemble. He placed the bamboo tube in front of the altar, burned incense, and showed it the utmost respect by prostrating himself before it. He then ordered the *weinuo¹* to strike him three times with the cane. All those present, both monastic and lay, gasped [in awe]. Because of the severe punishment, the assembly increased.

*In praise*:

Ah! Suppose nowadays someone were to send Daoan's package, the recipient would break the bamboo tube and rebuke him. How rare this is! Such a saintly master and sagely disciple, even from one thousand years in the past, I still praise the both of them.

### 4. Bearing a Load to Learn the Teachings

Jingtuo of the Sui dynasty was from Ji Prefecture. He became a monastic at an early age and was famous for his filial piety and integrity. When he went to learn the teachings, he would put his mother on one end of his shoulder pole and his sutras and brushes on the other. When it was time to eat, he would settle his mother under a tree and would enter the village to gather alms.

### 5. Skillfully Discussing Abstaining from Meat

Gunavarman of the Song dynasty was [formerly] a member of the royal house of Kashmir. In the eighth year of the Yuanjia era² he reached Jianye. The emperor asked, "I want to abstain from meat and killing, but this body rules a nation. I cannot do as I wish. What should I do?"

---

1. 維那: Officer in a Chan monastery responsible for discipline.
2. 元嘉八年: 431 CE.

He replied, "The practice of an emperor is different from that of a commoner. An ordinary man is of low position and name and must depend on his own hard work. For the emperor, all four seas[1] are his home and the people are his children. He speaks a single good word and the officials and commoners are happy. Through good government, man and the spirits are in harmony. By not taking life through corporal punishment or overworking the people through corvee labor, the wind and rain, heat and cold will be in harmony, and the hundred kinds of grain will flourish. Practicing vegetarianism in this way is great vegetarianism. Not killing in this way fulfills the precepts. If you fast for half a day to spare a single animal's life, how can that compare?

Touching his table, the emperor said with a sigh, "The common people are confused by profound teachings, and monastics are stuck on supramundane teachings, but from such words as the venerable's I have truly opened my eyes and fully understand. [Such teachings] reach across the human and heavenly realms!" He then ordered his officials to make offerings, and made Buddhism the state religion.

*In praise*

For emperors who do not believe in the Dharma, it is not just that they do not believe, but that the Dharma has not been explained in its full wonder and profundity. For example, Gunavarman's teachings were spoken perfectly: they are skillfully phrased, but do not violate the true Dharma. The true Dharma and mundane law can be integrated without hindrance.

---

1. 四海: The entirety of the world.

Those excellent moral advisors[1] of the past did not do more than this. Nowadays monastics are locked in their biased views, and always think they are righteous. They do not know that they allow the emperor not to wish to be close to monastics; but it is because of these people that it is so. Thus it is said that the earthworm knows nothing of the celestial dragon's transformations.

### 6. Suffering to Protect a Goose

In the time of the Buddha, a bhiksu went to beg at the door of a pearl seller. At that time, the seller was stringing pearls for the king. He placed the pearls to one side to get some food, but one of the pearls suddenly fell to the ground, where a goose swallowed it. As the pearl seller gave food to the bhiksu, he noticed that the pearl was missing, and suspected the bhiksu. To protect the goose, the bhiksu took the blows until he bled. The goose came to lick the blood, and the pearl seller's anger turned to the goose, which he beat to death.

The bhiksu felt sad and wept, the pearl seller thought that it was odd and asked him why. The bhiksu told him. The pearl seller understood, and, ashamed of himself, repented and bowed before the bhiksu.

### 7. A Letter of Recommendation in His Sleeve

Chan Master Xuedou Chongxian of the Song dynasty attained the Dharma under Guangzuo Zhimen. He then traveled through eastern and western Zhejiang. The Scholar Zeng said, "Lingyin

---

1. 諫議: Government post responsible for providing moral guidance to the emperor. In literature they are characterized as having unshakable integrity and speaking the truth to the emperor even if it puts their own lives in danger.

temple is one of the world's wondrous places, and Chan Master Shan is an old friend of mine," and provided Xuedou Chongxian with a letter of recommendation.

Chongxian arrived at Lingyin temple where he lived for three years amid the hustle and bustle of the community. At that time, the scholar Zeng was on a mission in western Zhejiang, and went to visit Chongxian. But no one in Lingyin temple knew him. At the time there were over one thousand monastics there. He asked someone to check the bed registry, and only then was able to find him. [Zeng] asked him where his letter of recommendation was. [Chongxian] removed it from his sleeve, and it was sealed just as he had left it. He said, "You are kind and caring, but I am a wandering monastic who makes no demands of the world. How can I submit this recommendation?" The scholar Zeng laughed, and Chan Master Shan was surprised.

*In praise*:

These days, when someone obtains a letter from an important official they treat it as if it were a large piece of jade. Day and night they try to profit from it. Apparently no one has heard the story of Xuedou Chongxian. I marvel at Xuedou Chongxian, who taught the tenets of his school like thunder and lightning, and was in no way inferior to Deshan or Linji.[1] In looking at his life his magnanimous bearing was out of the ordinary. As disciples of the Buddha, you must be self-respecting.

---

1. 德山 臨濟: Two celebrated ninth-century Chan masters known for teaching by shouting and hitting.

## 8. He Who Walked Among Woodcutters and Shepherds

Puyuan of the Tang dynasty was from Xinzheng in Zhengzhou. He received the teachings from Chan Master Dawei Dahui, and attained the Dharma under Venerable Master Mazu of Jiangxi. He held fast to his intelligence and concealed his glory such that it seemed that he did not speak at all. In the tenth year of the Zhenyuan era[1] he hung his staff on Mount Nanquan in Chiyang, where he wore a hat and clothing made of straw, fed cattle, associated with woodcutters and shepherds, and worked the mountain fields. He did not set foot off of Mount Nanquan for thirty years.

In the middle of the Taihe era[2] Prefect Chiyang, Ambassador Lu, and General Liu asked him to teach the Dharma. His teachings became popular and widespread. He was called the ancient Buddha of Nanquan.

*In praise*:

The patriarch Huiyun did not leave Mount Lu for forty years, Teacher Wang did not set foot off of Mount Nanquan for thirty years. This is the high virtue of the ancients. But all of this only comes after their minds awakened, it is not suitable for beginners. Those monastics who do not understand the great matter will be willing to travel thousands of miles to seek out teachers. Why is it that at this time we ignorantly meditate in one place and lose good opportunities? Chan master Zhaozhou was traveling at age eighty, Xuefeng climbed Touzi three times and nine times climbed Mount Dong. I dare to give this advice to those ignorant people who retreat in isolation.

---

1. 貞元十年: 794 CE.
2. 太和: 827-835 CE.

### 9. Fully Experiencing Hardship

When Tan Wujie of the Jin dynasty heard how Faxian and other monks personally went to India, he vowed to go even if it cost him his life. In the first year of the Yongchu era,[1] he set out from Changan with Tanlang and Sengmeng in a group totaling twenty-five people, and went west across the desert. There were no birds in the air or beasts on the ground. In the vastness surrounding them, they didn't know where they were. By watching the sun, they could determine east and west, while bones marked the way.

They arrived at the Congling mountain range, which was covered with snow, winter and summer. They encountered evil, poisionous dragons, and the wind rained down sand in torrents. Through the Himalayas they encountered a great river rushing between the eastern and western mountains, so they stretched across a rope to act as a bridge. Ten people crossed and once they reached the other shore they lit a fire as a signal. The next person coming behind knew the other had already crossed, and so made his way there. For a long time there was no sign of the smoke; they then knew that a strong wind had blown down the rope, knocking people into the river.

Crossing the Himalayas and the sheer precipices of the cliffs was fraught with danger. On one cliff there were old wooden stakes with facing holes which they used for their ascent, each with four stakes pulling themselves up and passing the stake back. After three days they reached level ground. They took stock of their numbers and found they had lost twelve people.

Heading off toward central India they found the way barren, and the only thing to eat was wild honey from rocky crevices. Another

---

1. 永初元年: 420 CE.

eight of the remaining thirteen died. Although confronted with so many dangers, Tan Wujie repeatedly recited Avalokitesvara's name.[1] Upon arriving in Sravasti[2] they encountered thousands of horrible elephants. They consigned their fate to Avalokitesvara. Suddenly a lion appeared and drove away the elephants. Arriving at the Ganges they encountered a herd of buffalo, and they consigned their fates as before. A large vulture scattered them. Later, in southern India, they returned to Guangzhou by ship, carrying the sutras they had collected.

*In praise:*
Reading accounts of those who in the distant past went west brings tears to the eyes. Each word and line of the sutras was acquired with sweat and blood. What a pity if someone treats them lightly, handles them with dirty hands, puts them in dirty places, possesses them without reading them, reads them without practicing them, or even worse uses them to win food and clothing or obtain fame and benefit.

## 10. Ringing a Bell to Alleviate Suffering

Zhixing of the Sui dynasty resided at the great Zhuangyan Temple, where he was a bell ringer. In the fifth year of the Daye era,[3] he lived with a monk by the name of Sansuo, who had a brother who, while accompanying the emperor, died on the road. [The brother's] wife dreamed of her husband who said, "I got sick at Peng City,

---

1. Avalokitesvara is the bodhisattva of compassion. To recite his name is to petition the bodhisattva for intercession.

2. 舍衛國: Ancient Indian city where many of the Buddha's discourses are said to have taken place.

3. 大業五年: 609 CE.

died, and fell into hell. I benefited from the bell of Zhuangyan Temple, which shook hell and liberated me. I would like to repay the kindness. Please offer ten bolts of silk."

His wife offered the silk, which Zhixing distributed to the monastics. They asked, "How can striking a bell have such an effect?" Zhixing replied, "When I ring the bell it is my wish that all the sages and saints come to the temple." He rang the bell three times. As he continued to ring the bell, he said, "It is my wish that those suffering in evil realms can hear the sound of the bell and be freed from their afflictions. I cannot shrink from my work even if in the bitter cold of winter my skin cracks and my hands bleed."

# MASTER OUYI

**Master Ouyi** (1599-1655) was a monastic from Jiangsu Province. In his youth he considered himself a Confucian and was openly opposed to Buddhism. At age twenty Ouyi's father died and he began chanting the *Ksitigarbha Sutra* in remembrance. The experience brought him to Buddhism and eventually lead him to the monastic life.

The selected calligraphy is written by contemporary painter and calligrapher **Dong Shouping**.

# The Base Man Projects His Faults on Others
## 小人以己之過為人之過

The base man projects his faults on others;
He always complains to heaven and blames others.
The gentleman sees the faults of others as his own;
He always examines and blames himself.

# MASTER MIAOXIE

**Master Miaoxie** was a fourteenth-century monastic from Zhejiang Province. In terms of lineage he was part of the Tiantai School, though he cultivated Chan meditation as well as Pure Land recitation practices.

In his "Treatise on the King of Treasures Samadhi," Miaoxie examines ten impediments to spiritual progress, and indicates how seeming obstructions can actually be beneficial.

# Treatise on the King of Treasures Samadhi
## 寶王三昧論

Do not ask for the body to be without sickness, for if the body is without sickness, greed and desire will easily arise.

Do not ask for a world without difficulty, for if the world is without difficulty, arrogance will arise.

Do not ask to investigate the mind without obstruction, for if there is no obstruction you will skip over what you have learned.

Do not ask to practice free from Mara, for practicing free from Mara weakens your vows.

Do not ask to make plans that are easily accomplished, for accomplishing things easily will lead you to despise determination.

Do not make friends that benefit yourself, for making friends that benefit yourself damages your morals and sense of justice.

Do not ask to live with others and be satisfied, for with satisfaction the mind becomes conceited.

Do not ask to give and have the favor returned, for if favors are returned then you will develop improper intentions.

Do not ask for others to share their benefits with you, for having benefits shared with you will lead to the mind moving falsely.

Do not ask to have your own oppression immediately removed, for if oppression is immediately removed anger will arise.

Therefore, the skillful teaching of the sages is to take sickness as medicine, obstruction as liberation, Mara as a Dharma companion, adversity as success, openness with others as a resource, betrayers as gardens and parks, spreading one's virtues as discarding shoes,[1] giving charity as prosperity, and oppression and being wronged as a way to practice. Taking the hard way can actually make things easy, while taking the easy way can in fact make things hard. The Buddha attained the Way of Buddhahood amid obstacles—even Angulimalya and Devadatta[2] who opposed him were prophesized by the Buddha to attain Buddhahood. Is it not that adversity may become ease, or the bad that is done to me return as achievement? Nowadays, if those who study Buddhism do not become accustomed to difficulty, then when difficulties arise they will not be able to sustain themselves and will lose the great jewel of the Dharma king. What a pity! What a pity!

---

1. 棄屣: Expression meaning to expect nothing in return.

2. 鴦崛魔羅 提婆達多: Two of the Buddha's early antagonists. Angulimalya was a serial killer who later reformed his evil ways after becoming a monk, and Devadatta was a monk who attempted to murder the Buddha and take control of the sangha.

# Tang Yin

唐
寅

**Tang Yin** (1470-1523), also known by the pen-name **Liuru**, was a painter, writer, and government official from Jiangsu Province. Though he is primarily remembered as a painter, he was also an accomplished poet. His poetry is compiled in the *Collected Works of Layman Liuru*.

# Song of a Life
一世歌

From time immemorial it is rare for a man to live          1
    to seventy,
Eliminate the years of childhood and old age and
There's not much left between,
Save frost and worries.
After mid-autumn[1] the moon lacks brightness.          5
After tomb-sweeping[2] the flowers lose their beauty—
Surrounded by flowers, under the moon, sing a song;
Make haste to fill the empty wine goblet.
There is so much money in the world that
    you cannot make it all;
There are so many positions in the court that          10
    you can't hold them all.
High position and plentiful money create worries,
Turning your hair prematurely white.
Spring, summer, autumn and winter;
    just a snap of the fingers,
The bell sees off the dusk; the cock announces
    the arrival of the dawn.
Gentlemen, look at those people who came before you:          15
We come once a year to find them buried by weeds.
How many tombs are among the weeds, high and low?
Each year, half of the tombs have no one to sweep them.

---

1. 中秋: Mid-Autumn Festival, an annual Chinese harvest holiday celebrated on the fifteenth day of the eighth lunar month.
2. 清明: Tomb Sweeping Day, an annual Chinese holiday to remember one's ancestors and tend to their graves.

# Yang Shen

楊
慎

Yang Shen (1488-1559), also known by the pen-
name **Shengan**, was an author from Sichuan
Province. Yang Shen was an accomplished writer,
poet, scholar, and playwright. He was also one of
the Ming dynasty's most prolific authors, and his
work has been widely collected in various com-
pendiums of period literature. Extant compilations
of his work include the *Lyrics of Shengan* and the
*Lyric Collection of Ten Thousand Choices.*

His poem "Rolling, Rolling the Yangze Flows
East" was so acclaimed that, during the Qing dy-
nasty, it was added as an epigraph to the classic
Chinese novel *Romance of the Three Kingdoms.*

# Rolling, Rolling the Yangze Flows East
*Tune: Riverbank Fairy*
滾滾長江東逝水

Rolling, rolling the Yangze flows east,                                          1
The waves washing away heroes.

Right and wrong, success and failure, all empty.
The green mountains remain,
How many red sunsets?                                                            5

White haired fisherman by the riverside,
Watching the autumn moon and the spring breeze;
A pot of unstrained wine welcomes me again.

How many events, from antiquity until now,
All are matter for our laughter and talk?                                        10

# WANG XIJUE

王
錫
爵

**Wang Xijue** (1534-1614) was a government official and scholar from Jiangsu Province. After
passing the imperial examination he eventually
became a Hanlin scholar in 1573. His writings are
collected in the *Works of Wan Wensu.*

# Foundations: Some Admonitions
## 本箴

Filial piety is the foundation for establishing self.                1
Loyalty and kind heartedness are the foundation of intention.
Resolve is the foundation for engaging in advanced studies.
Reading is the foundation for starting a family.[1]
Solemnity is the foundation for a proper family.                5
Hard work and thrift are the foundation for maintaining
    one's family.
Having few desires is the foundation for good health.
Cautious speech is the foundation for keeping out of
    harm's way.
Controlling one's desires is the foundation for getting rid
    of illness.
Honesty and prudence are the foundation of being an official.    10
Kindness is the foundation for the treatment of the people.
Choosing good friends is the foundation for gaining benefit.
Modesty is the foundation for receiving instruction.
Self-cultivation is the foundation for stopping slander.
Shouldering responsibility is the foundation for receiving       15
    blessings.
One sutra is the foundation for a child's education.
Storing good deeds is the foundation for enriching
    one's offspring.
Convenience is the foundation for handling affairs.
Expediency is the foundation for meeting contingencies.
Courage and strategy are the foundation for holding a post.      20

---

1. Reference to passing the imperial examination and receiving the steady salary of a government official.

Real victory is the foundation for gaining fame.
Saints and sages use the mind as their foundation;
The gentleman focuses his energies on these foundations.

# Qu Dajun

屈大均

**Qu Dajun** (1630-1696) was a writer and poet from Guangdong Province. Qu Dajun spent some time as a monastic, though he disrobed to pursue his literary career. His poetry is finely written, though it tackles heavy themes and promotes social consciousness. Qu Dajun had great concern for the plight of the common people.

His works include, *Writings from the Thatched Hut of Nine Songs* and *Writings from the Hall of Taking Hold of the Way.*

# Grieve for the Falling Leaves

*Tune: Dreaming of the South*

悲落葉

1  Grieve for the falling leaves;
The leaves fall, fall to make spring.

Every year, the leaves fly away and still there are leaves.
Every year people depart, leaving fewer people;
5  Upon the rouge there are fresh tears.

Grieve for the falling leaves;
The leaves fall, never to return.

Though they return, flowers cover the trees,
The new branches are not the ones in the past;
10  Slowly the water flows away.

# VI

1644–1911

# Qing Dynasty

# EMPEROR SHUNZHI

Empeor Shunzhi (r. 1638-1661) was the first emperor of the Qing dynasty. He is also known for his talents as a painter and poet. The emperor was a great patron of Buddhism. He renamed the "Golden Bell Hall" to the Buddhist-themed "Hall of All Goodness," and built a precept platform within the palace where he sponsored the ordination of 1,500 monastics.

In addition to supporting the sangha through imperial patronage, he often wrote of his wishes to become a monastic himself, though he was routinely dissuaded from doing so. His intentions can be seen in his poem, "In Praise of Monastics," where he not only celebrates the virtue and purity of the monastic life, but longs to enter it himself.

# In Praise of Monastics
## 讚僧詩

1  Food for all the monasteries in the world is piled as high
      as a mountain,
  Whenever you go with your alms bowl there is food to eat.
  Gold and jade are not dear,
  Only the monastic's robe is hard to wear.

5  I am charged with all the land, the mountains and rivers,
  Oppressed by concern for the nation and the people.
  For one hundred years, 36,000 days,
  Such cannot compare to the ease of half the day of a monastic.

  Arriving confused, departing ignorant,
10  This life lived in vain.
  Before birth, who was I?
  After birth, who am I?

  In adulthood, I am myself.
  When I close my eyes, who will I be?
15  It would be better not to have come, and therefore not have
      to leave;
  Arriving with joy, departing with sorrow.

  Joy and sorrow, meeting and parting, all are cause for anxiety.
  Who knows when the day of complete ease will come?
  If I can know the life of a monastic,
20  It would not be too late to turn back.

It's hard to compare a worldly life with that of a monastic:
Free from worries, free from anxieties—at ease.
The food is simple and pure,
One is always dressed in a monastic robe.

Traveling the five lakes and four seas as an honored guest      25
Because of *bodhi* planted in previous lives.
All are true arhats
Who wear the Tathagata's triple robe.

The golden bird and the jade rabbit[1] move from east to west.
To be human one must not scheme.      30
One hundred years of life is but a midnight dream,
The ten thousand miles of heaven and earth are as
    a chess board.

King Yu established the nine states,[2] King Tang sent
    King Jie into exile.[3]
Qin annexed the six kingdoms,[4] but the Han took over
    them all.[5]
So many heroes from time immemorial;      35
Now, burial mounds, from north to south.

---

1. 金烏玉兔: The sun and the moon.
2. First king of the Xia dynasty, who designated the first system of provinces.
3. First king of the Shang dynasty, who came to power by banishing the last king of the Xia dynasty.
4. First emperor of the Qin dynasty, who unified China by annexing the six states of Chu, Qi, Yan, Han, Wei, and Zhao.
5. The rise of the Han dynasty after the collapse of the Qin dynasty.

The emperor's yellow robe rather than the purple *kesa*,[1]
From a single thought of ignorance.
I was a monk in the west,[2]
40   How then was I born into the imperial family?

Eighteen years without freedom;
Fighting in the south, battles in the north—when will I rest?
Today I let it go, and go west,
For a thousand or ten thousand autumns, it matters not.

---

1. 袈裟: Formal outer robe of a monastic.
2. 西方: Relative to China, the west refers to India.

# MASTER YULIN TONGXIU

**Master Yulin Tongxiu** (1614-1675) was a monastic from Jiangsu Province. Ordained in the Linji Chan School, he was named National Master by Emperor Shunzhi in 1660.

The selected calligraphy was written by contemporary painter and calligrapher **Qiu Dafu**.

## Avoiding Meaningless Words
## 省虛文

Avoiding meaningless words, serve the sincere and respectful;
    this is true politeness.
Eschewing the superficial, practice thrift;
    this is true utility.
Distancing oneself from the cunning and fawning,
    draw close to the benevolent;
    this is true interaction.
Savoring the simple and the tranquil,
    feel shame in striving for things;
    this is true family customs.

# MASTER FODING

**Master Foding** (1647-1721) was a monastic from Hebei Province. Ordained in the Chan School, he was the abbot of Baiyun Temple in Henan Province (not to be confused with the modern day Baiyun Temple outside Beijing), and greatly expanded the temple to include over five thousand rooms.

## Baiyun Temple in Minquan County
### 民權白雲寺

The Buddha is in the Western Heaven,
    the Dharma flowing east;
Light shines across the four continents.
When the Buddha arises in the world the
    *nagas* and *devas*[1] rejoice;
When no monastics speak the Dharma,
    ghosts and spirits worry.

---

1. 天: Heavenly beings.

# LIN ZEXU

**Lin Zexu** (1785-1850) was a scholar and government official from Fujian Province. He is remembered as an example of highly moral governance, particularly due to his involvement in trying to suppress the illegal British opium trade. Lin Zexu not only found opium to be harmful, but the trade of China's valuable commodities to the British in exchange for what he saw as a poison for the Chinese people to be immoral.

The selected calligraphy is in Lin Zexu's own hand.

## Such Thoughts Which Are Unwholesome, Do Not Think of Them
### 念非善莫舉

1 Such thoughts which are unwholesome, do not think of them.
Such people who are unwholesome, do not associate with them.
That which you have not seen, do not speak of.
That which is unjust to receive, do not take.

5 When healthy, think of yourself as ill,
And you will protect yourself.
When wealthy, think of yourself as poor,
And you will protect your family.

# Zʜᴜ Bᴏʟᴜ

**Zhu Bolu** (1627-1698) was a writer and educator. His most famous work, *Aphorisms on Running a Household*, is a collection of maxims and moral guidelines that draws from both Buddhist and Confucian ideas of family and morality.

The selected calligraphy was written by contemporary sculptor and calligrapher **Furu**.

# Aphorisms on Running a Household
## (selection)
### 治家格言

Each meal of porridge, each meal of rice,[1]
Consider the difficulty for it to arrive here.
Half a bolt, half a thread of cloth,
Always remember that these arrive through difficulty.

---

1. 一粥一飯: Morning meal and evening meal. Collectively referring to all meals.

# Yunxian Shenquan

**Yunxian Shenquan** (1624-1684) was a poet and calligrapher from Shanghai. His style is graceful and flowing, and he is regarded as one of the most important calligraphers of the early Qing dynasty.

The selected calligraphy is in Yunxian Shenquan's own hand.

雲
閒
沈
荃

# Do Not Say That One Can Deceive with a Single Thought
## 勿謂一念可欺也

1   Do not say that one can deceive with a single thought;
Know that heaven, earth, ghosts and spirits are watching.
Do not say that a word can be taken lightly;
Know that there is eavesdropping all around.
5   Do not say that a matter can be handled neglectfully;
Know that family and life are related.
Do not say you can take advantage of a situation;
Know that fortune and misfortune will be visited on
    your descendents.

# ZHENG XIE

**Zheng Xie** (1693-1765), also known by the pen-name **Banqiao**, was a writer, painter, calligrapher, and government official from Jiangsu Province. He passed the imperial examination at an early age and served as prefect of Fan and Wei counties in Shandong Province. Both as an official and a writer he was known as being simple, kind, morally upright, and eccentric. His writing is collected in the *Complete Works of Banqiao*.

The selected calligraphy is written in Zheng Xie's own hand.

## Written on Bamboo and Rock
### 題竹石

Grab the green mountains in your teeth and
    never let go,
Fix your feet in the broken escarpment.
One thousand scrapes, ten thousand blows,
    and still resilient,
Bearing winds from all directions.

# One Filled with Pride Is Easy to Damage
## 滿者損之機

One filled with pride is easy to damage,
One lacking pride easily grows.
One's loss can benefit others.
Externally, others' temperament becomes calm,
Internally, one gains safety of mind.
Calm and safe, there is merit in this.

# Tao Tingjie

**Tao Tingjie** (1785-1856) was a scholar, calligrapher, and government official from Guizhou Province.

The selected calligraphy is written in Tao Tingjie's own hand.

# When Someone Speaks of Me
## 人之論我也

When someone speaks of me,     1
It's better to tolerate it than debate about it.
When someone insults me,
It's better to let it go than try to prevent it.
Do not be too harsh in chastising people for their     5
    unwholesomeness,
You must consider what they can endure.
Do not set the bar too high when teaching people
    wholesomeness,
You must consider what they are capable of achieving.

# LIANG YAN

**Liang Yan** (d. 1785) was a scholar, painter, and calligrapher from Anhui Province. His works include *Thoughts on Calligraphy* and *Notes on Painting*.

The selected calligraphy is in Liang Yan's own hand.

# Exposition on Wealth, Rank, Poverty, and Humility
## 富貴貧賤論

The morality of wealth is in giving.
The morality in poverty is not seeking.
The morality in rank is in serving those below.
The morality of humility is setting aside one's power.

# EMPEROR YONGZHENG

**Emperor Yongzheng** (1687-1735) was the fifth emperor of the Qing dynasty and ruled from 1723-1735. As emperor he was autocratic, and fiercely punished corruption within his court. He also did much to promote Buddhism, and was a student of **Master Jialing Xingying**. His writings include *Sayings from the Imperial Writings* and *Record of Selecting the Devil and Distinguishing Strange Things*.

His poem "Lines Describing Huiju Temple" shows a deep understanding of Chan Buddhism, and makes reference to **Master Mazu Daoyi's** teaching of "the mind is the Buddha, the Buddha is the mind."

## Lines Describing Huiju Temple
句容慧居寺

The mind is Buddha—this truth is not true.
There is no Buddha, there is no mind—
    these negations are false.
Try to overcome the duality of true and false by
    sitting in meditation.
Do not mention relying on the mind or the Buddha.

# VII

## 1911

# Republic of China

# MASTER HONGYI

**Master Hongyi** (1880-1942), born **Li Shutong**, was a prominent writer, artist, calligrapher, and, later, monastic from Zhejiang Province. As a young man Li Shutong studied Western painting and music at the Tokyo School of Fine Art. Later he returned to China and worked as a writer, journalist, and teacher.

In 1918 Li Shutong ordained at Daci Temple in Huangzhou, taking the ordination name Hongyi. He greatly admired the conduct of **Master Yinguang**, a contemporary of his, and emulated him by not becoming an abbot and not taking on any lay or monastic disciples, choosing instead to relate to others solely through his writing.

The selected calligraphy is written by **Wang Naizhuang**, a Chinese calligrapher, intellectual, and one of the founders of China's Society for Modern Calligraphy.

# True Friendship
## 君子之交

1 True friendship
Is as bland as water;
What one can order an elephant to take.[1]
Very close, yet one thousand miles away.
5 Ask me, what is proper?
Silence, and no words—
Flower branches are full of springtime;
Heavenly mind, full moon.

---

1. 執象而求: A very small quantity of water.

# I Do Not Know What It Means
# to Be a Gentleman
## 我不識何等為君子

I do not know what it means to be a gentleman,
But see that he is the one that receives the least.
I do not know what it means to be a base person,
But see that he likes to profit at the expense of others.

# MASTER TAIXU

**Master Taixu** (1889-1947) was a monastic and revolutionary from Zhejiang Province. Taixu was a leading voice in reforming the sangha and promoting Humanistic Buddhism. Though criticized by many during his life, his ideas and teaching methods went on to be embraced by many prominent twentieth century Chinese monastics.

Taixu's poem "Thoughts on My Fiftieth Birthday" specifically recounts a 1939 pilgrimage to Bodhgaya, India, the site of the Buddha's awakening. Taixu reflects on his own ideals and frustrations with the slow progress of reform, set against China's military struggles with Japan and the devastation wreaked upon its citizenry.

The selected calligraphy is in Taixu's own hand.

# Thoughts on My Fiftieth Birthday
## 五十生日感言

I was not born at the right time, and have                                        1
    one hundred worries;
This sadness and frustration has lead to many mistakes.
I left home long ago, and cut all ties with my family,
What is hard to forget? Kindnesses unrepaid.
Every birthday[1] reminds me of my mother,                                       5
My maternal grandmother possessed rare virtue.

Having left home and entered the sangha,
    my karmic connections broadened;
Teachers, friends, and followers are as thick as bamboo.
Witnessing the decline of Buddhism that I tried to save,
Desiring to reform the monastic order, I wondered,                               10
    how best to proceed.

Today the nation is devastated.
The people are abused and insulted; blood and tears flow.
The world is oppressed by the flames of evil,
Afflicted with disasters, one upon another.
Propagating the Dharma, I walked the whole nation,                               15
Traveling and teaching around the world;
The nation and the world are in dire straits.

I lead Buddhists to tour the Buddha's country.
All the Buddha's sons are powerful in mind and courageous,

---

1. 母難: Literally "Mother's Suffering Day," a Buddhist name for one's
birthday, to encourage gratitude towards one's mother for giving birth.

20 Looking askance at wealth as if it were floating clouds.
Honest and refined, Upasaka Tan[1]
Who brings together the cultures of India and China,
Wishes me long life on this, my birthday.

My life is but a bubble on the sea;
25 I wish that one bubble could lift a myriad of sufferings,
That the wishes of the people and the nation be fulfilled.
That the people of the world would stop fighting and killing,
Look at one another with compassion
    and throw down their weapons;
That this bubble bursts on a calm sea,
    universally blissful and safe,
30 The Buddha's light shining throughout the universe.

---

1. 譚居士: Tan Yunshan, a Buddhist scholar teaching in India and a contemporary of Taixu.

# Study Is Valuable for
# Knowing What Is Important
## 學貴知要

Study is valuable for knowing what is important,
Be not overly covetous.
Action is valuable at the appropriate time,
Be not mired in ancient ways.

# MASTER HSING YUN

**Master Hsing Yun** (b. 1927) is an author, monastic, and philanthropist born in Jiangsu Province. Ordained at the age of twelve, Hsing Yun has spent his life promoting Humanistic Buddhism through writing, charity, art, and developing Buddhist culture.

In 1949 Hsing Yun left China for Taiwan and began contributing to and editing Buddhist periodicals as well as publishing popular Buddhist works such as *The Song of Silence* and the novel *National Master Yulin.*

The selected poems are from *Humble Table, Wise Fare*, a collection of verses and aphorisms from Hsing Yun's talks and writings. The numbering of the poems correspond to the first volume of the Chinese edition.

# Humble Table, Wise Fare
## (selections)
### 佛光菜根譚

## [I.9]

Everything has its pros and cons,
Simply understand how to weigh them.
Always keep sight of what is possible,
Even dry stones and rotten wood can be
    used as medicine.
Everyone has strengths and weaknesses,
Simply understand how to bring out the best in others.
Always emphasize the merits of others,
Even broken copper and brittle iron can be
    forged into steel.

## [II.19]

You must have roots in your heart to be able to
    blossom and bear fruit.
You must have hope in your heart to be able to
    achieve professional success.
You must have the truth in your heart to be able to
    travel all over the world.
You must have principles in your heart to be able to
    stand true everywhere.
You must have virtue in your heart to able to
    tolerate all things.
You must have the Way in your heart to be able to
    embrace everything.

**[V.141]**

Cultivate to not haggle with others,
Cultivate to not compare with others,
Cultivate to handle affairs with courtesy,
Cultivate to smile at people,
Cultivate to not mind being at a disadvantage,
Cultivate to treat people kindly,
Cultivate to not have worries in mind,
Cultivate to speak well more often,
Cultivate to befriend virtuous people,
Cultivate so that everyone attains Buddhahood.
If everyone is able to accomplish these ten cultivations,
Everyone will enjoy a free and happy life in the
     Pure Land of the Buddha.


**[II.42]**

Life with suffering and happiness is abundant.
Life with success and failure is reasonable.
Life with gain and loss is fair.
Life with birth and death is natural.


**[II.59]**

Reforming the mind and one's nature
Is the remedy for changing your destiny.
Turning over a new leaf
Is the prescription for creating your destiny.


**[I.104]**

Give confidence to others, give joy to others,
Give hope to others, make things convenient for others—

Giving has limitless, wondrous uses.
Understand tolerance, understand peace,
Understand modesty, understand respect—
Understanding has limitless, wondrous meanings.

[II.130]
Learning to "pick it up" and "let it go"
Can expand the breadth of your mind.
Being able to see far ahead and do the right thing
Can elevate your life.

[III.37]
Life is like a seesaw,
If it's not up, then it's down.
Personal conduct is like a scale,
If it's not high, it's low.

[II.139]
Repentance is not just prostration of the body;
It is introspection of the mind.
Repentance is not just a moment of confession;
It is a lifetime of removing defilements.

[VI.126]
Convert temper into determination,
Convert emotion into intelligence,
Convert resentment into cordiality,
Convert anger into drive.

**[V.31]**

By preserving lives and not killing,
    one will naturally have longevity.
By giving alms and not stealing,
    one will naturally have wealth and position.
By being respectful and not engaging in sexual misconduct,
    one will naturally have harmony.
By honoring words and not lying,
    one will naturally have a good reputation.
By living a normal life and not taking intoxicants,
    one will naturally have good health.

**[IV.11]**

Don't bear any grudges, don't complain,
Then there will be less worry and less anger.
Don't fuss, don't compare,
Then there will be more help and more affinity.

**[I.4]**

By taking the short end of the stick, you can cultivate virtue.
By putting yourself in another's shoes, you can develop
    compassion.
By accepting things as they are, you can be carefree.
By enjoying without attachment, you can always be happy.

**[IV.112]**

By making concessions, there is endless, vast sky.
By yielding a little, how leisurely it is.
By tolerating a few words, one is without worry and at ease.
By being able to endure, one is happy and carefree.

**[III.47]**
Patience is the first rule of personal conduct.
Courtesy is the first rule of dealing with all things.
Modesty is the first rule of saving one's own skin.
Openness is the first rule of being considerate.

**[I.136]**
Get along in harmony with all people.
Make good use of money.
Be sparing with clothing and food.
Make body and mind pure and dignified.
With affection be selfless and elevated.
Be one with nature, in mutual respect.

**[II.149]**
With people, do good deeds and speak good words;
Follow wholesomeness as flowing water to be a good person.
Be perfectly willing to do good deeds;
For everyone to be happy, keep good thoughts.

**[IV.101]**
Tolerate one sentence and the roots of misery
    have no place to sprout.
Forgive one thing and no longer fight others
    to be greater or lesser.
Endure one moment and extreme difficulty
    becomes a white lotus pond.
Make one concession and that is the road of
    cultivation in this world.

**[V.131]**
Do not reject callously, rejections should provide
some alternatives.
Do not reject rudely, rejections should provide
some flexibility.
Do not reject bluntly, rejections should be artful.
Do not reject angrily, rejections should be given
with a smile.

**[VI.50]**
If the four great elements do not work in harmony,
People will have sickness in their bodies.
If people encounter obstacles,
They will have sickness in their minds.
If people insult others with abusive language or lies,
They will have sickness in their mouths.
If people are unpleasant to others,
They will have sickness on their faces.
People who practice Buddhism
Should not allow their body, mouth, and mind to
become sick.

# MASTER XUYUN

虚
雲

**Master Xuyun** (1840-1959) was a monastic from Hunan Province. He received full ordination at the age of twenty under **Master Changkai**. Xuyun spent the first decades of his long life as a monk traveling throughout China, Tibet, Burma, India, and Sri Lanka, learning and living in seclusion.

At the age of fifty-six, while on retreat at Gaomin Temple in Jiangsu Province, Xuyun had the enlightenment experience described in his poem "The Cup Falls to the Ground." After hours of meditation, an attendant was filling Xuyun's teacup and spilled boiling water on his hand, knocking over the cup. Xuyun would recall the moment the cup hit the floor as the moment of his enlightenment.

Xuyun continued to travel and teach, becoming a unifying figure in Chinese Buddhism, and was instrumental in improving the relationship between the Buddhist sangha and the Chinese government following the revolution.

## The Cup Falls to the Ground
### 杯子扑落地

The cup falls to the ground,
The sound sharp and distinct.
The universe is shattered;
The crazed mind calms.

# MASTER YINGUANG

**Master Yinguang** (1862-1940) was a monastic from Shansi Province. He is generally considered the thirteenth patriarch of the Pure Land School, and was the leading proponent of Chinese Pure Land Buddhism of the twentieth century. Ordained at the age of twenty-one, Yinguang spent most of his monastic life living in seclusion at Mount Putuo, communicating to those who sought his teachings in letters. His letters contain personal admonitions and encouragements to practice with a mastery of Buddhist and Confucian scripture.

In 1918 his correspondents collected and published excerpts from these letters which were received with much acclaim. Despite increasing fame, he remained largely cloistered for the rest of his life.

The selected calligraphy was written by **Master Longlian**, a twentieth-century monastic, scholar, and occasional calligrapher. Dedicated to fostering female Buddhist leaders, she established the College for Buddhist Nuns in the 1970s.

# Though Others Do Not Return
# the Good I Do
## 縱人負我德

Though others do not return the good I do,
I take it as myself not returning the good of others.
I feel shame for not doing enough for all people,
Such that there is nothing to regret.
So that the cruel and despotic
Have no means to arise.

# MASTER MANSHU

**Master Manshu** (1884-1918) was a writer, painter, and monastic. Born in Yokohama, Japan the son of a Cantonese merchant and a Japanese woman, his father returned to China in 1903. Shortly thereafter, Manshu ordained at age twenty.

Manshu wrote widely, including popular works like *The Lone Swan*, regular contributions to the *People's Daily*, and Chinese translations of western works such as *Les Miserables*.

# A Letter to Tiaozheng[1]
## 寄調箏人

This Chan mind has evoked jealousy from the beauty;
The Buddha said, in the end, even our enemies are family.
With bamboo hat and cape, I return,
Without love or hate for anyone.

---

1. 調箏: One who tunes stringed instruments. In this instance it refers to a specific woman who was a good friend of Manshu.

# MASTER CIHANG

**Master Cihang** (1895-1954) was a Buddhist monastic in the Humanistic Buddhist tradition of **Master Taixu**, having studied under him at the Minnan Buddhist Studies Institute. Rather than seek structural or political reform, Cihang primarily sought to champion a renaissance in Buddhist education, culture, and learning.

Following Japan's return of Taiwan to China in 1945, Cihang was invited to Taiwan by **Master Miaoguo** and there founded the Taiwan Buddhist Studies Institute. Starting in 1949, many monastics began to flee China for Taiwan due to the rising tensions on the mainland, and Cihang expended great effort in harboring and protecting them. These activities were mistaken as aiding communists by the authorities and Cihang was imprisoned, spending more than one hundred days in jail.

# Posthumous Admonitions
## 遺偈

1   I urge all disciples: constant reflection is of great importance;
   Every day we think and act, examine how much is
      wholesome or unwholesome.
   Only if you feel at peace are east, west, south,
      and north all well;
   If but one person is not liberated you cannot run away!
5   Dharma nature is inherently tranquil, cause and effect
      do not miss, even a little;
   As you sow so shall you reap, nobody can stand in for you.
   A temple is as a sky flower, or the moon in water.
      May you establish good everywhere and at all times.
   I wish you to broadly form wholesome karmic connections,
      to better save yourself and others early.

# Zhang Daqian

**Zhang Daqian** (1899-1983) was one of the most celebrated Chinese painters of the twentieth century. Zhang had a great love of classical Chinese painting, including the Buddhist-inspired styles of the Tang and Song dynasties which he emulated in much of his work. In addition to evoking classical styles in his own painting, Zhang's superb craftsmanship and attention to detail allowed him to be a master forger, producing art forgeries from many periods and styles that are nearly indistinguishable from authentic paintings.

The selected calligraphy is in Zhang's own hand.

## Speaking the Dharma,
## the Blue Lotus of Nine Platforms
### 說法青蓮九品臺

Speaking the Dharma, the blue lotus of nine platforms,
Heaven knows of the sickbed and the groaning
By chance one smiles and the Chan mind
　　will be set on meditative concentration.
From nowhere, Ananda[1] comes.

---

1. 阿難: Great disciple of the Buddha. He was the Buddha's attendant, and is said to have committed all the Buddha's discourses to memory.

# MASTER BINZONG

**Master Binzhong** (1911~1958) was born in Taiwan to a wealthy and prominent family. He ordained despite the disapproval of his family by running away from home at the age of fourteen. Feeling that there was no proper Buddhism in Taiwan he left for China in 1933 to study under the eminent monastics of his day. He returned to Taiwan in 1939 to teach the Dharma and later constructed Fayuan temple in Xinzhu.

The selected calligraphy was written by **Juehai Shanren**.

# Dharma Words
## 法語

Study and you can receive the merit of peace
and harmony for life.
Study Buddhism and create more joyful connections
with others.

# VIII

# Temple Couplets

# Temple Couplets

Buddhist Temples are as much a part of China's Buddhist heritage as the generations of monastics and volumes of writings. The structures of Chinese temples are commonly adorned with calligraphy of poetic couplets. Some couplets are adapted from Buddhist sutras, while others are original compositions, often of anonymous authorship.

佛寺聯語

### 1. Jinshan Temple at Zhenjiang
Ages of heroes like waves have disappeared,
Of the famed mountains, most are monasteries.

### 2. Dinghui Temple at Zhenjiang
All before me are karmically connected,
    Becoming close, becoming friends,
    Why would by heart not be filled with joy?
So many unbelievable things in the world,
    One sows, one reaps,
    Why not have a big belly filled with tolerance?

### 3. Guangji Temple at Wuhu
A big belly is able to tolerate,
    Tolerate all under heaven
    That is difficult to tolerate.
An open mouth can laugh,
    Laugh at those people in the world
    You are able to laugh at.

### 4. Rongchuang Temple, Suzhou
Noble teachings, famous sayings,
    Individual joy cannot compare with joy shared.
Buddhism's objective,
    Freeing life is better than taking life.

### 5. Tiantong Temple of Yin County
A great Dharma protector does not see a monastic's error,
Good Dharma friends are able to tame emotions.

## 6.  Lower Tianzhu Temple, Hangzhou

The Dharma banner presents clouds of loving kindness.

Looking at the autumn moon and spring flowers,
All filled with profound truth of the three kinds of emptiness.

The lamp of wisdom hangs above the treasure seat.[1]

Hearing the morning bell and evening drum,
They are nothing but a bit of Chan.

## 7.  Upper Tianzhu Temple, Hangzhou

Rough and rugged is the way of the world;

Watch the confused people spur
Themselves up the mountain,
Struggling for advantages
On cliffs with no way back.

Compassionate is the Buddha and Heaven;

Wishing that sentient beings
Turn their heads and find a safe harbor,
And quickly cross the sea of suffering
In the boat of loving kindness.

## 8.  Upper Tianzhu Temple, Hangzhou

In the mountains birds sing and the flowers are fragrant.

Heaven's vibrant ways,
Inclines one to seek the wonderful truth.

On the lake the breeze is fresh, the moon is white.

The scenery is truly empty,
This is the Tathagata.

---

1. 寶座: The seat from which monastics teach the Dharma.

### 9.  Taoguang Temple, Hangzhou

Sound of pines, sound of bamboo,
   Sounds of bells and gongs,
   All sounds at ease.[1]
Scenes of mountains, scenes of water,
   Scenes of mist and rosy clouds,
   All scenes are empty.

### 10.  South Putuo Temple, Xiamen

Manifest the body at ease,
   Wish that all sentient beings together board
   The boat of loving-kindness
   And quickly cross the sea of suffering.
Liberate future *kalpas*,
   Hope that the Buddha rains the Dharma widely
   And vigorously turns the tide.

### 11.  Putuo Temple

One at ease,
   One contemplating,
   Contemplating at ease.
Come thus,
   See thus,
   See the Thus Come One.

### 12.  Putuo Puji Temple

Heaven and earth allow me calm,
Fame and advantages make a person busy.

---

1. 自在: This is a reference to 觀自在, the Chinese name of Avalokitesvara, the bodhisattva of compassion.

### 13. Putuo Puji Temple

The evening bell and the morning drum
  Wake the world's famous
  And privileged people.
The sounds of the sutras and the Buddha's name
  Call back the dreamy, confused people
  From the sea of suffering.

### 14. Seven Pagoda Baoen Chan Temple, Zhejiang Province

The Tathagata speaks *prajnaparamita*,
  Where is the sutra?
  There is a pagoda.
Sentient beings initiate the mind of supreme bodhi,
  Wholesome Dharmas increase,
  This repays the Buddha's kindness.

### 15. Seven Pagoda Baoen Chan Temple, Zhejiang Province

The ten directions come,
    The ten directions go,
    Together the ten directions accomplish
    The ten direction's affairs.
Tens of thousands of people give,
    Tens of thousands of people donate,
    Tens of thousands of people are all tied,
    To tens of thousands of peoples' karmic connections.

### 16. Kaibao Temple, Kaifeng

Do nothing that is unwholesome,
    Do all that is wholesome,
    One already understands the Tathagata's true teaching.

The four great elements are inherently empty,
The five aggregates do not exist,
That is the heart of the paramitas.

### 17. Kaibao Temple, Kaifeng
The forty-eight vows[1] universally include all varieties of people,
Certainly, if ten thousand practice,
Ten thousand people will be reborn there.
The twenty-five existences can all be reborn with right faith,
One should form each thought on the Tathagata.

### 18. Dharma King Temple, Dengfeng
Be a good person,
The mind will be upright,
The body at ease, and the spirit calm.
Do some good deeds,
And become known by heaven
And earth and ghosts and spirits.

### 19. Dharma King Temple, Dengfeng
Take one step back,
Heaven is higher and the earth broader.
Yield a little bit,
The mind becomes even and the temper calms.

### 20. Ciyun Temple, Tianzhen
As long as Hell is not empty I will not become a Buddha.
When sentient beings are all liberated, bodhi will be attained.

---

1. 四八願: The vows of Amitabha Buddha.

### 21. Guangsheng Temple, Zhaocheng

Effects have causes, causes have effects,
 If there is an effect, there is a cause.
 Whichever cause is planted, such will be the fruit.
The mind is the Buddha, the Buddha is the mind,
 There is mind, there is Buddha.
 If you wish to seek Buddhahood, first seek the mind.

### 22. Yongquan Temple, Fuzhou

There is no need to sweep the pure land.
There is no need to close the door of emptiness.

### 23. Linyang Temple, Fuzhou

Porridge goes, rice comes,[1]
 Don't let time cover your face.
The bell rings, the board sounds,
 Always be mindful of life and death.

### 24. Mountain Gate, Fo Guang Shan

Ask once, where am I going today?
Think thrice, when will I return?

### 25. Venerable Zhongyang's Memorial Hall, Fo Guang Shan

A real man of flesh and blood practices the Buddha's vow to
 liberate the world.
With our youthful ideals and integrity we follow the patriotic
 spirit of Venerable Zhongyang.

---

1. In a monastic environment, porridge is typically eaten in the morning, and rice is typically eaten for the midday meal.

## 26. The Non-Duality Gate (outside), Fo Guang Shan
The Buddha liberates all beings,
>    All varieties of sentient beings
>    Achieve supreme enlightenment.
His light reaches all Dharma realms,
>    Transcend at once and directly see the Tathagata.

## 27. The Non-Duality Gate (inside), Fo Guang Shan
This gate is called "non-duality,"
>    Duality or non-duality, both are one's true face.
This mountain is Vulture Peak,
>    Mountain or no mountain, nothing is not my pure body.

## 28. Main Shrine, Fo Guang Shan
Tusita and Saha come and go,
>    The *vajra* throne is unmovable.
Pure Crystal and Ultimate Bliss to the left and right,
>    Both equally respected as Dharma kings.

## 29. Great Compassion Shrine, Fo Guang Shan
Across the Saha world;
>    One thousand hands,
>    One thousand eyes,
>    Infinite manifestations.
Traveling the lands in ten directions;
>    Great loving kindness,
>    Great compassion,
>    Liberating sentient beings as numerous as sand in the Ganges.

### 30. Great Wisdom Shrine, Fo Guang Shan
Once the ancient Buddha's teacher,
  The self-proclaimed Dharma prince.
Now the Tathagata's attendant,
  People call him Manjusri.[1]

### 31. Longevity Shrine, Fo Guang Shan
The Dharma wheel is always turning, crossing the sea of suffering
Take the vow to return and liberate sentient beings.

### 32. Longevity Shrine, Fo Guang Shan
Always recollect parental kindness,
  Today we are karmically connected,
  Today may they be liberated.
Inherently there is no hell,
  This mind creates it,
  This mind can destroy it.

### 33. Dining hall, Devotee Building, Fo Guang Shan
If one eats what is prepared,
  Consider the difficulty for it to arrive here.
If one speaks of things after the fact,
  Be weary that you too would be confused in such a case.

### 34. Main Gate, Hsi Lai Temple
From the east the Buddha's light shines
  Universally upon the three thousandfold world system.
Coming west the Dharma water flows
  Continually throughout the five continents.

---

1. 吉祥: The Bodhisattva of wisdom.

### 35. The Five Bodhisattva Hall, Hsi Lai Temple

The five sages share the same mind and open the Pure Land.
The sevenfold assembly cooperates and protects the temple.

### 36. Weituo[1] Shrine, Hsi Lai Temple

The general heeds the calls of the three continents,
His treasure staff subdues Mara's armies in the six realms.

### 37. Qielan[2] Shrine, Hsi Lai Temple

From the east, from the west,
    Both Qielans protect the temple.
In the past, in the present,
    His virtue and majesty intervene everywhere.

### 38. Library, Hsi Lai Temple

The Buddha sun grows brighter,
    Heavenly flowers are radiantly resplendent.
The Dharma wheel always turns,
    The palm leaves speak the sutras.

### 39. Meditation Hall, Hsi Lai Temple

Meditate in the shadows of the stars,
Bring the body to ease among the clouds, water, and light.

### 40. Memorial Pagoda, Hsi Lai Temple

The Buddha, the Tathagata, liberates all from suffering.
Good men and women ascend the nine levels of the lotus terrace.

---

1. 韋馱: Deity that protects Buddhist temples.
2. 伽藍: Deity that protects Buddhist temples.

### 41. Mountain Gate, Fu Shan Temple

Together ascend to the land of merit,
  Ten thousand practices,
  Ten thousand people go.
The mountain gate is straight ahead,
  One thought,
  One Tathagata.

### 42. Main Shrine, Fu Shan Temple

Cultivate merit and wisdom together,
  Broadly forming good conditions.
These mountains and forests are beautiful,
  Universally liberate sentient beings.

### 43. Flower Ornament Shrine, Yuan Fu Temple

The palm leaves of the Buddhist canon
  Speak Manjusri and Samantabhadra's minds.
The rain of flowers and clouds of incense
  Are offered to Vairocana and Sakyamuni Buddha.

### 44. Main Shrine, Fu Guo Temple

Who first awakened from the great dream?
  Turn your head back sooner,
  And believe the Western Pure Land really exists.
Long have I admired the hero's wind,
  In time one lets go
  And realizes the essence is truly empty.

### 45.  Tower of Five Meditations, Hong Fu Temple, Guiyang

If the five contemplations are understood,
>   Even gold is easy to digest.
If the three minds are not realized,
>   Even water is difficult to digest.

### 46.  Longquan Temple, Changle

He is the great king of doctors,
>   Able to skillfully cure sentient beings of all their afflictions.
He is the wondrous Dharma torch,
>   Suddenly breaking the six realms of existence and their
>   shroud of beginningless ignorance.

### 47.  Guiyuan Temple, Hanyang

From past till present, how many religions have come?
>   Free and equal, none compare to the Buddha's.
From east to west, countries and civilizations advance,
>   Their noble ideals yield to the Dharma king.

### 48.  Jinyun Temple, Chongqing

You may know this body cannot last long,
>   Why all this rushing, all this busyness,
>   Doing bad things?
But I understand all past lives have their destiny,
>   Only all this purifying, all this cleansing,
>   Can make one a good person.

### 49.  Wuyou Temple, Yueshan

Handle affairs without the mind,
>   All may be happy.

Be a person lacking character,
>One cannot be at ease.

## 50. Qian Fo Chan Academy, Emei

A world is contained in a grain of rice;
The universe can be cooked in half a wok.

## 51. Yuantong Temple, Kunming

The Buddha's light shines universally on the earth,
>Plant melons and harvest melons,
>Plant beans and harvest beans,
>Cause and effect is the truth.

The Dharma wheel always turns in the human world.
>Wholesome deeds have wholesome results,
>Unwholesome deeds have unwholesome results,
>Gods upon the altar.

## 52. Guanyin Hall, Xiangshan Temple, Zunyi

A single color, a single incense
>Offered to the ten direction of Tathagatas,
>The lotus world is adorned with infinite vows.

One thousand hands, one thousand eyes
>Liberate sentient beings from suffering.
>The Saha World is filled with the mind of great compassion.

## 53. Monastery Gate, Famen Temple, Fufeng

Enter this gate and let go of everything:
>All people attain great benefits.

Ascend to the Buddha land, and look around as you like:
>Each one's nature is pure and refined.

### 54. Baita Temple, Lanzhou

Cut a patch of cloud to mend a monastic's robe;
Invite the bright half moon to read the sutras.


### 55. Flowing Cup Pavilion, Tanzhe Temple

Water flowing over the stones: motion is still.
The mountain appears amid the clouds: illusion is real.


### 56. Majestic Hall, Guangde Temple

Teach the three vehicles,
    Broadly embrace all beings
    And ascend the road to enlightenment.
Hand down the Dharma for thousands of years,
    Universally liberate all beings and realize *bodhi.*


### 57. Yonghe Lamasery, Beijing

Through coming together the earth took shape,
    It is not an unconditioned phenomena.
Sentient beings share the same essence,
    One should hold such a view.


### 58. Manjusri Hall, Jinding Temple, Mt. Jizu

See it, then do it,
    Do it, then let go,
    All done, what is not done?
Wisdom arises from enlightenment,
    Enlightenment arises from ease,
    All arisen, they have not arisen.

### 59.  Guangxiao temple, Taizhou

For ten years the river flows east,
>For ten years the river flows west,
>Don't let time slip away.

One foot in the door,
>One foot outside,
>Be careful of where you step.

### 60.  Kaiyuan Temple, Quanzhou

The Buddha is sentient beings' compassionate father.
The precepts are your great teacher.

# List of Authors and Calligraphers

# Index of Titles and First Lines

# Glossary

**aggregates, five** (五陰): The Buddhist analysis of five elements that make up the self: form, feeling, perception, mental formations, and consciousness. The five aggregates are commonly cited for the suffering that their existence incurs on living beings.

**Ananda** (阿難): Great disciple of the Buddha. He was the Buddha's attendant, and is said to have committed all the Buddha's discourses to memory.

**Angulimalya** (鴦崛魔羅): A monastic disciple of the Buddha. Before he became a monastic he was a serial killer who attempted to murder the Buddha. After meeting the Buddha he mended his horrific ways.

**astrological cycles** (周星): A twelve-year revolution of the Chinese zodiac.

**Avici** (阿鼻業): The most terrible and severe level of the hell realm. Beings reborn in Avici hell are said to live there for many *kalpas* and endure unceasing pain and suffering.

**bodhi** (菩提): Transliteration of the Sanskrit term for enlightenment. Also used as a modifer for many terms associated with enlightenment, such as "bodhisattva."

**Bodhidharma** (菩提達摩): The monastic who brought the Chan School of Buddhism to China during the sixth century. He is considered the twenty-eighth Indian patriarch, though the reckoning of Chinese Chan patriarchs restarts, with him being considered the first. Accounts of his life are highly legendary, and his actions and motivations are common subjects of Chan writing.

**bodhisattva** (菩薩): A type of Buddhist practitioner associated with Mahayana Buddhism who has vowed liberate living beings and become a Buddha. The term "bodhisattva" is used both to describe people beginning on the path who have made the initial aspiration, as well as the exalted sages of Buddhism who have nearly attained Buddhahood.

**Buddha** (佛): A fully enlightened being. When unqualified, it often refers to Sakyamuni Buddha, the founder of Buddhism. In literature the Buddha is often described as a very tall man with a golden, radiant complexion and is given various names and epithets.

**Buddha nature** (佛性): Concept that enlightenment is possible because all living beings inherently possess the potential to become Buddhas, and the only reason they do not realize this potential is because one's Buddha nature is obscured by affliction.

**Caoxi** (曹谿): Location where Master Huineng, the sixth patriarch of the Chan School, taught. Caoxi is also used to refer to Huineng himself.

**child of the Buddha** (佛子): The expression "child [son] of the Buddha" has several definitions, with varying levels of expansiveness. It may refer to (1) a monastic disciple of the Buddha, (2) any disciple of the Buddha, or when given as a plural, it commonly refers to (3) all living beings.

**Classic of Filial Piety** (孝經): One of the Confucian classics which collects several dialogs examining filial piety.

**Devadatta** (提婆達多): A monastic disciple of the Buddha and the Buddha's cousin. Devadatta is characterized as a wicked man who was jealous of the Buddha and wished to seize control of the sangha. He attempted to murder the Buddha several times and created schisms within the sangha.

**devas** (天): Celestial beings made of light that reside in the heavenly realms of rebirth.

**Dharma** (法): Multi-faceted term that refers to the teachings of the Buddha, as well as the truth of the universe.

**Dharma king** (法王): Another name of the Buddha.

**dharma realm** (法界): Buddhist doctrinal term that refers to the true nature of reality as experienced by enlightened beings.

**Dharma wheel** (法輪): Symbol for the Buddha's teachings. The Dharma wheel is also commonly used to describe the act of the Buddha teaching the Dharma, most specifically the moment when he taught for the first time and "set the wheel of Dharma in motion."

**Dharma-declining age** (末法): Period many years after the Buddha passes away when authentic Buddhist teachings no longer exist. Many Chinese Buddhist thinkers write from the perspective that they are currently living in this age.

**Dharmakaya** (法身): One of the three "bodies" or aspects of the Buddha. The Dharmakaya is the aspect of the Buddha that pervades all of existence. To "realize the Dharmakaya" is also a common synonym for attaining enlightenment.

**dhyana, eight states** (八解): Successive stages of meditative absorption. The first four signify ever deepening states of tranquility, while the last four refer to formless states, including the states of infinite space, infinite consciousness, nothingness, and neither thought nor non-thought.

**directions** (方): When given as a set of four, they refer to the four cardinal directions, and many elements of Buddhist mythology are organized by these four directions. When given as a group of ten the term specifically refers to the four cardinal directions, the four intermediate directions, plus above and below, though is more generally used to refer to "everywhere."

**door** (門): Common symbol for the Buddhist teachings, most commonly used to refer to the multitude of different teaching methods or skillful means.

**elements, four great** (四大): Earth, water, fire, and wind. The Buddhist analysis of the totality of physical existence.

**extremes, two**: Used throughout Buddhist writing to denote various extremes, such as existence and emptiness, and *nirvana* and samsara.

**eyes, five** (五眼): Five special types of perception which a practitioner gains through cultivation: the physical eye, the celestial eye, the wisdom eye, the Dharma eye, and the Buddha eye.

**Felai Peak** (飛來峰): One of the highest points on Mount Wulin. Home to many Buddhist temples and Buddhist rock-face relief sculptures.

**finger pointing at the moon** (執指為月): Commonly cited metaphor for people mistaking provisional teachings for ultimate truth. It is a reference to a passage in the *Suramgama Sutra*: "One points a finger at the moon to show people. Such people should follow the finger to see the moon. Those who mistake the finger for the moon not only lose the moon, they lose the finger."

**Flower Adornment Sutra** (華嚴經): One of the largest and most celebrated sutras in Mahayana Buddhism.

**flowers** (花): A symbol of feminine beauty, or of the impermanence of life.

**gate** (門): *See* **door**.

**golden bird** (金烏): Poetic name for the sun.

**Golden Lotus Treasure Realm** (金蓮寶界): Another name of Amitabha's Pure Land.

**ground** (地): A particular stage of a bodhisattva's cultivation.

**guest** (客): When the speaker refers to himself as a "guest," it commonly means that they are no longer in a position of power or comfort.

**Guwen movement** (古文): Tang dynasty literary movement headed by Liu Zongyuan and Han Yu which sought to return to the direct, expressive writing of the Han dynasty and eschewed the florid diction and structures that were popular at the time.

**Haoli** (蒿里): Land of the Dead. The name is a reference to a fabled cemetery in the southern foothills of Mount Tai.

**impurities, five** (五濁): Time, views, afflictions, beings, and life.

**jade rabbit** (玉兔): Poetic name for the moon.

**jin** (斤): Ancient Chinese unit of mass equal to roughly 500 grams.

**Jisai** (雞塞): Poetic way of referring to the border or frontier of a particular country.

**kalavinka bird** (頻伽): Mythic bird said to inhabit the Pure Land.

**kalpa** (劫): An Indic unit of time measurement. A *kalpa* is an incalculably long period of time spanning the creation and destruction of the universe.

**karma**: Buddhist teaching of cause and effect in which wholesome or unwholesome acts of body, speech, and mind have an effect on a being's future happiness and rebirth.

**kesa** (袈裟): Formal outer robe of a monastic.

**kindness, four** (四恩): The kindness of parents, teachers, one's country, and sentient beings.

**leaving home** (出家): Expression for ordaining as a Buddhist monastic.

**li** (里): Ancient Chinese unit of distance. The *li* varied throughout China's history, but can be considered roughly half a kilometer.

**Linji** (臨濟): Prominent Chinese Chan monastic and founder of the Linji School of Chan Buddhism. He is known for his style of employing shouting and hitting while teaching.

**lion** (獅子): Symbol for the Buddha teaching the Dharma.

**Lotus Sutra** (法華經): Major Mahayana sutra in which the Buddha asserts that all his previous teachings were only provisional teachings designed to lead beings to make the aspiration to become Buddhas.

**lower realms, three** (三塗): A subset of the six realms of existence in Buddhist cosmology. The beings reborn in the three lower realms have more negative karma than those born as human beings. These realms include the realm of animals, the realm of hungry ghosts, and the hell realm.

**Mahakasyapa** (迦葉): One of the ten great disciples of the Buddha, and the first Indian Chan patriarch.

**Mandarin duck** (金鴨): Symbol for marriage, as Mandarin ducks mate for life. The image suggests a newly wed couple.

**mani pearl** (摩尼珠): A mythical pearl capable of fulfilling wishes. In Buddhist writing it is used as a symbol for the incredible value of the Buddha's teachings.

**Mara** (魔): A malevolent being that embodies desire and is an adversary of the Buddha. The name is also used to refer to mental qualities that impede spiritual progress.

**Maudgalyayana** (目連): Great disciple of the Buddha known for his supernatural powers and great filial piety.

**Maya, Queen** (摩耶): Sakyamuni Buddha's mother.

**meats, three** (三牲): Beef, pork, and mutton. Commonly given as offerings in Chinese ancestor rites.

**mid-autumn festival** (中秋節): An annual Chinese harvest holiday on the fifteenth day of the eighth lunar month.

**mind seal** (心地印): Often discussed in the Chan School, the "mind seal" is the approval and confirmation of a student's enlightenment by an enlightened teacher. It is also sometimes used to refer to the teachings themselves.

**moral advisor** (諫議): A Chinese government official responsible for providing moral guidance to the emperor. In literature they are characterized as having unshakable integrity and speaking the truth to the emperor even if it puts their own lives in danger.

**Mount Lu** (盧山): Mountain in northern Jiangxi Province. Its beauty has inspired generations of Chinese poets.

**naga** (龍): Mythological serpent-like creature that lives in water.

**natures, five** (五性): Ordinary people, *sravakas* and *pratyekabuddhas*, bodhisattvas, indefinite, and "outsiders," meaning non-Buddhists.

**offerings, four** (四事): Clothing, food, shelter, and medicine.

**organs, five** (五內): Heart, lungs, liver, kidneys, and stomach.

**orifices, nine** (九竅): Both eyes, both ears, both nostrils, mouth, anus, and urinary tract.

**original vow** (本願): The vow to become a Buddha.

**outflows** (有漏): Afflictions. Called "outflows" because one's virtues escape by flowing out of them.

**outsider** (外道): A term used to refer to non-Buddhists.

**paramitas** (波羅蜜): Set of virtues accumulated over many life-times that allow one to "cross over" and become a Buddha. The paramitas are most commonly describes as a set of six virtues: giving, morality, patience, diligence, meditative concentration, and *prajna* wisdom.

**perfections**: *See* **paramitas**.

**poison dragon** (毒龍): Symbol for mental affliction.

**poisons, three** (三毒): Greed, anger, and ignorance. They are the elements from which all unwholesome conduct stems.

**powers, five** (五力): Five important virtues of Buddhist practitioners: faith, diligence, mindfulness, meditative concentration, and wisdom.

**prajna** (般若): Sanskrit term meaning wisdom, though in Chinese it is often used to specifically describe the transcendent wisdom of Buddhism. Also used to reference the *prajnaparamita* sutras, a class of Buddhist sutras concerned with the teachings on emptiness and non-duality.

**profound objective** (玄旨): A term used throughout the Buddhist sutras, though most prominently in the *Lotus Sutra*. It refers to the reason why the Buddha arose in the world.

**Qiang** (羌): Chinese minority group that lives mostly in northwestern Sichuan Province.

**railing, leaning against** (倚闌干): Commonly used image of remorse and regret. The image suggests looking out at nature from a balcony.

**realms, six** (六趣): A grouping of possible destinations of rebirth in Buddhist cosmology named for the type of beings that inhabit them. The typical set of six includes the hell realm, the realm of hungry ghosts, the animal realm, the human realm, the *asura* realm, and the heavenly realm.

**Red Cliffs** (赤壁): Site of a decisive battle during the Three Kingdoms period; a period whose generals and military heroes have since been immortalized in literature and the popular imagination.

**Sakyamuni Buddha**: Siddhartha Gautama, the historical Buddha and founder of the religion we know today as Buddhism. "Sakyamuni" means "sage of the Sakyans," which was the Buddha's clan name.

**sangha** (僧): The Buddhist monastic order.

**sarika bird** (舍利): Mythic bird said to inhabit the Pure Land.

**seas, four** (四海): The northern, eastern, southern, and western seas. Term used to refer to the entirety of the world.

**sense object**: Anything that can be cognized by the sense organs to create consciousness. Usually six sense objects are listed, corresponding to the six sense organs: form, sound, smell, taste, feeling, and *dharmas* (the sense object associated with the mind).

**Six Perfections**: *See* **paramitas**.

**sky flowers** (空華): Commonly used as a metaphor for things which are illusory, it specifically refers to the spots that appear in one's vision due to optical disorders.

**Sravasti** (舍衛國): Ancient Indian city where many of the Buddha's discourses are said to have taken place.

**suchness** (真如): Refers to the world just as it is, without being altered or filtered by perception. Perceiving suchness is a goal of Buddhist practice.

**Suddhodana, King** (淨飯): Sakyamuni Buddha's father.

**supernatural power, six kinds** (六般神): Miraculous powers possessed by great practitioners said to derive from their cultivation. Commonly given as a group of six, they include teleportation, celestial vision, celestial hearing, mind reading, knowledge of past lives, and destruction of all afflictions.

**sutra** (經): Buddhist text that records the teachings of the Buddha. As an object, the sutras themselves are often revered, and the production of sutra texts is considered meritorious.

**sutra case** (函經): A long, narrow container used to hold Buddhist sutras for chanting.

**Tathagata** (如來): Anothter name for the Buddha, and the one most frequently used by the Buddha to refer to himself. In Chinese *rulai* means "thus come," while the Sanskrit *tathagata* has the double meaning of "thus gone" as well. The name refers to the fact that, given the Buddhas understanding of reality, he cannot be said to truly come or go anywhere.

**Tathagatagarbha** (如來藏): *See* **Buddha nature**.

**ten thousand** (萬): Commonly used to express an infinite number, or refering to everything of a given category.

**tomb-sweeping day** (清明節): An annual Chinese holiday to remember one's ancestors and tend to their graves.

**treasures, seven** (七寶): Gold, silver, lapis lazuli, crystal, ruby, pearl, and carnelian. The seven treasures are commonly mentioned when describing superlative acts of generosity, as is found in the *Diamond Sutra*.

**Triple Gem** (三寶): The Buddha, Dharma, and Sangha, who are the enlightened teacher, the enlightened teaching, and monastic community. The central object of veneration in Buddhism.

**ultimate bliss** (極樂): Reference to Amitabha's Pure Land.

**unborn** (無生): Synonym for *nirvana*.

**unconditioned** (無為): Synonym for *nirvana*.

**vajra** (金剛): A mythical material that is indestructible, commonly used as a symbol for things which are steadfast or resolute. It can also refer to a mace-like weapon made from such a material.

**vehicle** (乘): In a Buddhist context, "vehicle" refers to various goals of practice, commonly given as groups. When mentioned as three vehicles, they usually refer to the goal of a *sravaka*, a *pratyekabuddha*, and a bodhisattva. When mentioned as two vehicles it refers to the goal of *sravaka* and *pratyekabuddha*, though more generally the term is used pejoratively to refer to those who are not bodhisattvas and do not embrace Mahayana Buddhism. When mentioned as "one vehicle," it is typically a reference to the *Lotus Sutra*, in which the Buddha teaches that the three vehicles are merely a provisional teaching to encourage beings to pursue the goal of becoming Buddhas.

**vihara** (蘭若): Simple monastic dwelling. Hermitage.

**water burial** (水葬): Burial practice attributed to several Chan masters. Through deep meditation they discern that they only have moments left to live. They then take a small boat out to sea and break a hole in the hull, sinking the boat. This is done so that others will not have to care for their bodies after death.

**waterway** (渠): Symbol for Buddha nature. Buddha nature is often described as the source of a river.

**Way** (道): In a Buddhist context, used to refer to the path of Buddhist practice. To "attain the Way" is synonymous with enlightenment.

**weinuo** (維那): An officer in a Chan monastery responsible for discipline or conducting the ritual affairs of the main shrine.

**west** (西方): Used to reference India, the birthplace of Buddhism, and Amitabha Buddha's Western Pure Land, where many Buddhists seek to be reborn after death.

**wind** (風): When used in conjunction with a person, that person's "wind" describes the influence of that person's virtuous conduct.

**wisdom, four** (四智): Four supramundane types of wisdom described in Yogacara philosophy and said to be gained by Buddhist practitioners as they cultivate their consciousness: the wisdom of perfect conduct, the wisdom of profound insight, the wisdom of universal equality, and perfect mirrorlike wisdom.

**wooden fish** (木魚): A bulbous woodblock-type instrument used in Buddhist liturgical chanting.

**Yellow River** (黃泉): The Chinese underworld.